BUILDING CAREER SUCCESS

ANTHONY JACKS

Legend Business Ltd,

107-111 Fleet Street, London, EC4A 2AB

info@legend-paperbooks.co.uk | www.legendpress.co.uk

Contents © Anthony Jacks 2018

The right of the above authors to be identified as the authors of this work has been asserted in accordance with the Copyright, Designs and Patents Act 1988. British Library Cataloguing in Publication Data available.

Print ISBN 9781787198180

Set in Times. Printing managed by Jellyfish Solutions Ltd

Linnet Mattey | www.linnetmattey.com

CONTENTS

FOREWORD

In today's feverish world of work the odds are against a long and successful career unless you plan ahead by identifying where you want to get, the direction of travel and how best to strengthen and deploy your skills. In this instructive and absorbing book Patrick Forsyth distils from his own experience and packages the street smart wisdom he has gained into practical advice of value to everyone from those starting out in their first job to those in mid-career and those in senior positions hoping to reach the top. *Building Career Success* is an important addition to Legend Business's Smart Skills series. It is congruent with and supplemented by other texts on behavioural skills such as business writing and negotiation.

No job today is secure and those who stand still without honing their skills or extending their competence will not move up the ladder in their organization and are vulnerable. The message of this book is therefore that career development is neither an option nor the simple pursuit of ambition. Patrick identifies the importance of honest self-analysis as a first step on the path to building a career and at every stage in the journey forward involving assessment of your skills, the additional qualifications you need and your work and personal non-work values. You will also need at some stage in your development to face up to the issue of how effective you are as a manager.

Other chapters in the book focus on people power, including the sensitive topics of networking, helping others and office politics; and the power of communication, including the ability to present, participation at meetings, fluent writing, thinking before you speak and, essentially, listening. Being effective also involves being open-minded, taking a creative approach, doing what is expected of you and honouring the commitments you make. In that way you will be seen to be good and do well in your organization.

For all of us who achieve success without much forethought and on whom Lady Luck has shone favourably we tend to take the credit while those who do less well tend to blame "bad luck" for our failures. As Patrick points out in the first chapter, even when we do well good things could probably be better if we had recognized and addressed lost opportunities. That is a sobering thought for the self-satisfied who may have thought that they knew it all and is the reason why everyone in employment should read this book.

Jonathan Reuvid

INTRODUCTION

Life is what happens when you are making other plans.
John Lennon

The above quotation encapsulates a painful thought. All too often, we are conscious of things happening to us. If they are good things, we are most apt to take them in our stride, either putting them down to our underlying brilliance, or "good luck" but, if they are not good, we blame "bad luck" rather than our own lack of foresight. In the latter case certain things are, with hindsight, clearly predictable and may lead swiftly to our sighing, "If only...". Similarly, good things that occur may also represent lost opportunities; they are good but could have been better. If we are ready for them or if we are "quick enough on our feet", then we can take more advantage of them.

At the same time, there are some things that we plan, like going away on holiday, and others which we may not see as plannable, almost as we do not try to control tomorrow's weather. Your career is amongst those important aspects of your life which you will want to influence. It is also something you cannot realistically make go exactly as you want. But that is no reason for not taking any action possible to make it go as near as possible to the way you want. You must not let perfection be the enemy of the good. In other words, just because you will not be Chief Executive tomorrow if you snap your fingers and shout "Promotion!" is no reason for not working at those factors that can take you in the right direction. And, as we shall see, there are many such things.

This book is not about the initial process of obtaining a job (though certain elements involved in so doing crop up along the way), it is about planning where you want to go and taking action, both in the way you work in your current job and by other means to ensure you make progress. Such progress may be measured in terms of position, of rewards (financial and otherwise), recognition, responsibility and authority. Everyone will see this in their own way. For some, the trappings of office are more important than to others. For some, money is the only measure. However you measure it, your ability to achieve what you want is not, in the real world, only a question of competence. There are organisations the world over with many people working in them who could do well in a more senior position. (There are also some who are in senior positions and not carrying out their responsibilities very well, and many more who will never rise above a certain level for all their good work. When most people would claim a degree of ambition, what is it that differentiates between those who do well and move up an organisation, who hold management positions and move on to the senior levels, and others who do less well?

Competence is clearly one factor, but there are others. Some of the additional factors are concerned with skills, some with perceptions - how people are seen – whatever they are, they create a total picture that combines to influence the likelihood of an individual making progress. It is these factors that this book reviews. It does not offer a magic formula. If there was a magic way to ensure that you became rich, famous, irresistible to the opposite sex and Chief Executive overnight, you would not find it in a book at this price! But you *can* increase the chances of success, and you may be able to increase them significantly.

Of course, it may be that any progress cannot be made without thought and effort, these are nearly always necessary if anything worthwhile is to be achieved. But the very fact that many different factors are involved increases the possibilities of your being able to swing the odds more in your favour. Everyone is likely to do better and progress more certainly if they think about it. Of the many things that are referred to in this book some can give *you* an opportunity to make a difference. What is more, the development of a career is essentially a competitive process. Most organisations have a pyramid shaped structure and, as the old saying has it: "There are more Indians than Chiefs." You need to appreciate the most common factors; these are things which anyone prepared to spend a little time and effort can achieve, because if you lag in these areas you allow potential advantage to go by default. And you need to find other things which your abilities and outlook allows you to excel in, so that overall you are able to create the right climate for progress.

Career development is not an option, nor is simply being ambitious. In today's competitive workplace environment, beset as it is with pressures of all sorts, active career development is essential. Doing nothing towards sorting out where you are going and how you will get there, not even thinking it through, is a sure recipe for missing opportunities and doing less well than may be possible. This book aims to help you think career development through in the right way, and to give you some specific ideas and advice as to what works best. Thereafter it is up to you. In every sense, the greatest asset you have in developing your own career is *yourself*.

CHAPTER 1
FIRST PRINCIPLES

ADOPT THE RIGHT OVERALL APPROACH

In the introduction, the point was made that there is no magic formula which can guarantee that you enjoy a successful career. Here we discuss what may seem a general point, yet it is probably as close to such a magic formula as exists. Career development is an active process. You have to work at it. That is not to say that you have to do nothing else. In fact much of what needs to be done is an integral part of the work you will be doing, only needing a "career development" focus on it as well as whatever other role it has in your business life, to be useful.

Any career is influenced by a thousand and one different factors. The organisation you work for, the people you work with and for, and the differing circumstances of each, all affect how you will progress. You cannot possibly predict everything that will occur along the way. What you can do is have a clear idea of the things that will help you as time goes by, so that you can keep a hand on the tiller. Being prepared to work at it is the first step (you see the need or you would probably not have purchased this book), but you cannot do so in a vacuum. Some analysis of you, your situation and prospects is helpful. Also useful, if not essential, is a plan; something that can be drawn from the analysis.

Both are investigated in a moment. So, the starting point is an appreciation of the necessity for career development, a resolve to work at it systematically that becomes a habit, and then an ongoing study of how you can make a difference and the application of any individual methods that you judge suit your circumstances.

Most often, the people you hope to emulate have not reached their positions by good fortune. Of course, good luck may have had something to do with it, but it is not something you should rely upon – just sitting back and hoping for a lucky break is *not* career planning – and, if and when it does arrive, it needs to be taken advantage of, developed and made permanent. The only element you can guarantee will always be there to assist you, is you. So think of yourself as an active careerist and go on from there.

DECIDE WHAT QUALIFICATIONS YOU NEED

It is said that you cannot have too many qualifications. To an extent this is true, though there are those who become perpetual students and never seem in danger of escaping into the real world at all. Here I want to say something about getting the balance right. First, let us put on one side those qualifications which are mandatory for particular fields of activity; for example if you wish to be an accountant, you have to pass the necessary exams. There is no decision to make here. If you want to get into a particular field, you must do the exam.

On the other hand, many qualifications are much less specific. How do you know, in advance, what an MBA will do for you, for instance? Such qualifications can be useful. They are not however, from an employer's point of view, any guarantee of competence (in my own field of marketing, there are certainly people with paper qualifications in the subject who have no marketing flair at all). Qualifications do of course, give some signs, namely they:

- Impart a great deal of knowledge
- Improve thinking (developing approaches to, say, problem solving)
- Develop skills, though usually much less than gathering knowledge (certain courses blend different elements very well, as with many programmes nowadays that combine a management degree with language study)
- Give you a "label".

It is this last point that needs some thought. Different qualifications are seen in a different light. This applies to both the qualification and to the institution from which it comes. There is a compromise to be made here for those at the stage of seeking qualifications – where will you be accepted? Where geographically do you want to be? How long is the course? What are the financial considerations? And so on. This kind of consideration is even more difficult if you are contemplating a post-graduate qualification, perhaps one that needs a break from work or private funding. When employers talk about what they want from their employees, they tend to link closely together "qualifications and experience" – this is what goes on a C.V. also – and they do go together, in other words whilst you are studying you do not get any work experience and vice versa. Part time courses exist to mix the two factors, but you may find the perception of them is also different from full time equivalents. So another balance that must be struck is between what advantages you will gain from, say a year working, and the same year spent on something more academic.

One more point: there is also a fashion element in how some of these things are regarded, with one institution seeming to be in favour at one moment, then another. All in all, you need to think long and hard about what will suit you best. What will give you the greatest career advantage in terms of both what you will learn and how the qualification will be seen? Then make a decision remembering both the saying that "you cannot have too many qualifications" and the various practicalities.

Note: not least here there are financial decisions to be made; gaining qualifications can be expensive and leave you in considerable debt, something that may inevitably affect you decisions as you seek employment.

INSIST ON A JOB DESCRIPTION

This is obvious and important; and curiously I regularly come across people and organisations where the whole area of job definition (and appraisal, which is touched on later) is ill-defined or non-existent. First, it is important from the point of view of any organisation. If managers are to manage, and manage effectively, then the organisation structure and who does what must be thought through, agreed and documented; and the whole process must link with the corporate objectives centrally and at the level of individual divisions or departments. What is more, whatever the formal benefits of a system of job definition, evaluation and appraisal (and they are undoubtedly a vital tool for personnel and other considerations) are – or should be – working documents, which act as a guide to individual managers and staff in day-to-day operational terms. You will gather that I am in favour of job descriptions.

But consider it too from the individual's point of view. Surely everybody wants to know whether they are doing a good job or not – a sense of achievement is after all, a basic human motivation coming from any work. How can you possibly gauge if you are being successful if the job in question is ill-defined? It is not possible and thus leaves a sense of dissatisfaction. More important still from the point of view of career development, progress in a career is perhaps, more than any other single factor, dependent on performance, and other people need a clear view of what this is in your case. As the old maxim has it, "you must never confuse activity with achievement", progress is so often dependent on *evidence* of achievement and that in turn is dependent on knowing what is expected of you and comparing how things go with this. A job description should not be restrictive, indeed it should be dynamic and if it needs changing and updating regularly so be it. It is after all, a working document.

So, in any job you do, make sure you have a clear, written, job description. I would go further: you should have one, everyone who reports to you should have one and whoever you report to should have one. In fact, the whole process works best if your staff see yours, and everyone else's, and you see the job description for your boss. That way everyone knows not only what everyone else is doing, but how the various responsibilities interrelate.

OBTAIN THE RIGHT REWARDS

Job satisfaction is desirable, important and makes the inevitably less attractive parts of any job worthwhile; but it will not pay the rent. Whatever you do, you no doubt expect a fair reward for it. Fair in this context, normally means a comparison with your peers in the same organisation and with those in comparable organisations such as your direct competitors in the commercial world.

A moment's thought shows that money is important in a number of different ways. It is a means of purchasing basic needs (and less basic needs too for that matter!). It is a symbol of the worth the organisation places on someone, it is a means of comparison, as stated above, and a reward in itself. But it is not the only reward. Most executive jobs involve increasingly complicated remuneration "packages" where in addition to the salary you may receive:

- A company car
- Incentive or bonus payments

- Share options
- Special terms loans
- Expenses (that do more than cover the costs incurred in conducting business on behalf of your employer)
- Discounts on company products or services (which will be more valuable in, say, an airline than in a firm manufacturing sewage treatment equipment or some such)
- Health and other insurance
- Group incentives (e.g. attending an overseas conference)

Some of these may well be linked to performance, and there may be more which you can think of that are favoured in your work field. Fashions vary with regard to such benefits and current practice tends to vary in different countries and change over time (as with company cars, much favoured in UK but nowadays being made much less valuable because of the way they are treated for tax).

Two further points need to be made here. First, do consider other rewards which should perhaps be weighed in the balance. For example, one job may pay less in the short term and yet offer unique training advantages that make it the best choice for the short term.

Secondly, do not be afraid to negotiate these kinds of benefit. Certainly once you reach a certain level, most organisations expect the package to have some element of tailoring. If you do not raise certain issues they may not get an airing at all. Similarly you may want to expand the agenda and include things the company have never even thought about previously. One example of this: an acquaintance of mine seconded to Singapore from London was offered but felt no need for a car in such a small place, but to keep himself mobile he negotiated a company motorbike! The difference in cost he took as money which suited him well and demonstrates useful flexibility. A final, warning point: negotiation is fine but you may come to a point where it is better and more valuable to your future career not to push further but maintain good relations with those with whom you are negotiating. Principles do not pay the rent, and in some economies it is a real risk to push things so far that your job becomes in doubt.

Note: it may be going beyond my brief, but the question of professional advice is worth a word. First, there could be occasions when you might sensibly check the terms of a contract with a professional. Secondly, whatever financial rewards you obtain, you may need advice about tax and savings and investments during your career.

TAKE A CHANCE

Here, I am not advocating an approach that throws caution to the wind, and you must consider your temperament and approach to risk, but chances do sometimes have to be taken. There is an old saying that says: "Don't be afraid to go out on a limb if that is where the fruit is." Trees are high and climbing may be dangerous, but it makes a fair point. You need to consider this in several ways:

- *Perception:* How do you want to be seen within your organisation? At one end of the scale, there is out and out recklessness which may be linked in the mind with such characteristics as being unthinking or taking ill-considered action. Such an image may be wrong for you. So too may be that of a staid, predictable and perhaps, as a result, less innovative person. You must consider where on the scale you should be, and even so can make the occasional exception.
- *Job skills:* The degree of taking a chance is something that you have to think about in terms of your job and the action and decisions it demands you take. Some decisions are a risk, and not everything goes right for companies and the people who work in them. Research,

consideration and careful decision-making must usually precede any significant action but there is still a place for a chance to be taken. A reputation for a reliable business instinct is good for anyone's image, but when this is there it is usually balanced by sound homework.

- *Career decision:* I know of people who have taken awful career decisions and gone through a bad patch as a result, and a few who have become stuck in something which they dislike or at least to which they are indifferent. Equally you may be put off a course of action because of the risk, or what you see as a step into unknown territory, and the fear of that clouds the argument in favour. In my own case, setting up my own business was the best thing I ever did in my career (my mistake, before anyone thinks I am claiming perfection, was not doing it earlier) - but it was also certainly the riskiest.

So you must balance security and good sense, care and consideration in decision-making with those other occasions when you have finally, as it were, to close your eyes and step out into the unknown. If you open them and find you are where you want to be it is very satisfying. Though it will not always be the right thing to do, or work out if you do it, taking a chance is likely to be something you have to do on occasion. Take the right ones and they can surely jump your career ahead.

GET IT IN WRITING

Far be it for me to suggest that employers are not to be trusted, but, realistically, some are not trustworthy. This may be a small number and it may be for reasons of error or ineptness more than it is vindictive, but it is worth taking note of and indeed the road to the law courts is populated by people who have not done so. Circumstances change; a simple agreement made with the Managing Director and owner may be worth little five years later when the company has been sold to a multinational conglomerate without a single scruple in any of its many parts.

The moral is that you should have written (and contractual) agreement to your appointment and the terms and conditions that accompany it. Assured by the publishers that this book will be on sale throughout the world, I will not go into the detail of employment legislation which varies a good deal in different locations. Suffice to say you should check what makes sense in the environment in which you work (checking twice as carefully if you plan to work in a foreign country), and insist on something appropriate in writing. The following items may contribute to the contract:

- The details in a letter of appointment
- A statement of terms and conditions
- Contents of collective agreements, rules, etc. (in some cases agreed with a Trade Union or employee body of some sort)
- The customs and practice of the organisation
- Statutory protections (those applying locally).

You should think broadly about what suits your circumstances and allow for any special situations. For example, if you are or become a director you may wish to have a written list of your legal and financial obligations. You may also feel more comfortable to have a note of any "standing instruction" relating to a range of things from expenses to how a company car may be used. Most of the time such documents are not operationally necessary; if problems or disagreements crop up however, they can be invaluable.

DO NOT BE LED BY EVENTS

One of those (often American inspired?) business terms that now pervade the English language is the word "Proactive", everything seems to need a proactive approach or a proactive process. Whatever happened to "active"? Perhaps the emphasis here should be on the reverse – do not become unthinkingly responsive.

Consider: you have set clear objectives, you have a plan and have thought it all through – then something happens. It may be anything – someone leaves the company unexpectedly, there is a merger or takeover, a new development, overseas expansion or even a death. It is certainly something you could either not have allowed for in your planning, or something which would have been very difficult to predict in terms of when it might occur. This kind of thing will often need to prompt rapid thinking, but may less often necessitate rapid action. Of course, there may be times when unless an opportunity is grasped very fast it will be gone. In this case, there still needs to be some thinking even if it must be less in depth and even more rapid. You do need to consider all the odds or you may find yourself repenting at leisure. The first task is perhaps to consider whether the urgency is real or apparent.

We all have 20/20 hindsight. It is always easy to look back and judge if something was right or wrong. However, it may be rather different at the time when facts may be limited and the outcome much less clear. I am not sure I can offer a definitive route through this kind of circumstance, except to say most decisions are better and more sure if given a little real thought, and that the temptation to take a risk in case an opportunity is missed forever is great. Perhaps doing your homework – the analysis and planning I have advocated – makes it more likely that you will be able to make good decisions rapidly when the need arises, in which case it is another reason why such planning is worthwhile. Otherwise, what seems like a good idea at the time can lead you badly off track and away from your plan and intentions; and that may work out or it may not. An active approach that includes real planning is more likely to cope with the real world and allow you to deal with any random factors in a way that is most certain to further your career aims.

BE OPTIMISTIC

I have a theory (entirely unbacked by any statistics!) that optimists tend to do better than pessimists or those who inherently worry about everything. Of course, you must never rely only on "waiting for something to turn up," but if you plan your life and career practically, taking the kinds of views, approaches and actions advocated in this book *and* do so in an optimistic way, that is not only better - you are likely to be more comfortable with it also.

DEALING WITH SUCCESS

Yes, having talked about optimism in the last section, I think it is right to deal with success early on in the book. The point I want to make is a simple one: do not broadcast your success in an arrogant or unpleasant way. However much you may admire successful people (and want to emulate them), those who crow about their success are almost universally resented. Modesty is a virtue. As Oliver Hereford said: "Modesty: the gentle art of enhancing your charm by pretending not to be aware of it," and there is sense in this, for understatement can be more powerful, especially when an overpowering approach can have the reverse effect of what is intended.

This is true of major factors, like significant promotion, and of smaller successes; no one likes someone who is always crowing just to score points. This leads us to another related point: promotion can mean you are working with people as your subordinates with whom you used to work as colleagues. This can be awkward for both parties, or at least it can feel awkward, and you have to work out a way of dealing with this situation. The right balance is important.

You probably can no longer be "one of the gang" as it were, but may find it useful to remain sufficiently close to take advantage of the best of the old relationships (importantly without playing favourites) whilst creating a new basis for the majority of your dealings with the people concerned. If your success is significant, people will know without your overdoing the hype; some self-publicity is helpful to a career, but it must never be such that it is perceived as arrogant, and by implication, putting others down.

Having set the scene we will now move on to the ideas and approaches that characterize active career development.

CHAPTER 2
SELF-ANALYSIS

CREATING A FOUNDATION FOR ACTION

The earliest "career plan" I can remember having in mind for myself when I was still at school, was to be an astronomer. This was born of a passionate interest in the subject rather than any link with my actual or likely abilities. However, once I began to check out what might be necessary, realism soon set in and, though my interest continues, my career took other paths. Career planning, perhaps sadly, does not mean conjuring up plans that are no more than pie in the sky, but proceeding on a clear, accurate and honest assessment of what might be possible.

This means looking inwards.

KNOW YOURSELF

Though we all like to think we know ourselves, this may not be entirely true. It is easy to make assumptions, to leave key elements out of the picture and so, as a result misjudge how our current profile lends itself to career progress, and just what sort of progress may be possible. Assumptions can link to past experience, fears, bad experiences or a host of things. An example of just how much we may misjudge ourselves perhaps makes the point: as a trainer, I conduct courses designed to improve peoples' formal presentations skills. One category of person who attends (usually told to attend by their employer) has never done this, or done very little of it, hates the thought of it because they know they cannot do it well and would much prefer to avoid the whole subject and the task. Yet these same people, or certainly many of them, prove to be quick and effective at learning how to do a good job on a presentation. They find there is a difference between not knowing how to go about something and inherently not being able to do it. With the knowledge of how to tackle it, and with practice, this can be added to their list of skills. Yet previously they may have been avoiding tasks, jobs, even promotion, that was likely to put them in a position where they would have to do this seemingly worrying task.

There may well be aspects of your nature and ability you think about in this way, so the first step to deciding a route forward is to look at where we are at the moment. This should be done systematically and honestly and you may find it useful to keep some notes of what the thinking produces. The next several sections lead you through a suitable progression of self-analysis.

ASSESS YOUR SKILLS

You might be surprised at how many skills you have. Remember that it is quite possible that things you do and take for granted, you can only in fact do because of considerable, and perhaps unusual, experience. So all the things for which you have aptitude you should list. Some general headings under which to group your abilities may be:

- **Communications** – everything from writing a report to issuing instructions
- **Influencing** – that includes persuading, negotiating and promoting ideas

- **Managing** – everything to do with managing other people
- **Problem solving** – analysing and drawing conclusions and coming up with solutions
- **Creativity** – generating ideas, seeing things in the round, having an open mind
- **Social skills** – not just relating to people but having insight, helping others, facilitating
- **Numerical** – figures, statistics, accounts, etc. and, these days, computers
- **Special skills** – here such skills as speaking a foreign language, unusual technical skills, etc. should be mentioned

At any stage of your career, you should have the full picture in mind and therefore documented. It would be an interesting exercise to list such things now or progressively as this section continues, and again when you have read the whole book. Some of the topics listed above will reoccur as we proceed and you may view things differently after a review of how important some of the skill areas are from a career point of view.

ASSESS YOUR WORK VALUES

It is not enough to know what skills you have. These must be viewed in the light of your work values. Do you, for instance, have a:

- Strong need to achieve
- Need for a high salary
- High interest requirements of work
- Liking for doing something "worthwhile"
- Desire to do something creative
- Or specific requirements (such as to travel, to be independent, innovative or part of a team)?

A wide range of permutations may be involved here and they may change over time. For example, travel may be attractive to the young and single but less so to people who have young children and then become more attractive again when a family is older.

ASSESS YOUR PERSONAL CHARACTERISTICS

Most people do not change their habits and ways, at least not dramatically and certainly not without effort, once they are old enough to be into a career. You need to assess yourself in this respect and do so honestly. Are you innovative, positive, optimistic, hard-working, prepared to take risks? What sort of a person, in fact, are you? There may be a clash here. In thinking through your work values you feel that you may be suited to, and want to be involved in, something with considerable cut and thrust, innovating, creative and generally working at the leading edge. But, an honest assessment of yourself may show that, whatever the superficial or status attraction of this option, it is just not really you. If risk taking is not your thing, then a different, perhaps more supportive, role is where you are likely to excel most.

ASSESS YOUR NON-WORK CHARACTERISTICS

One way or another, work and social life have to coexist alongside each other. They may do so peaceably, or there may be conflicts between them. It is not automatically necessary to career success to be a workaholic, though a strictly 9 to 5 attitude to the job is perhaps not recommended either. And on the positive side, work and interests or hobbies may overlap constructively, the one teaching you something about the other. There are questions to be asked here too:

- What are your family circumstances?
- Where do you need to live?
- How much time can you spend away from home?
- What are your other responsibilities and interests?

Family: If you have a partner, wife or husband then priorities may need to be set, because career-building priorities can clash. It is, sadly, perfectly possible to arrive successfully at the top of the heap – a success in business, but with home, family and happiness in ruins. This may sound dramatic, but the issues here are worth some serious thought. Not least, there are times when career decisions must be made fast or opportunities will be lost. If the relationship between home, family and work have never been discussed, then the man who comes home from the office to tell his wife: "I have this great new opportunity with the company, but it means living in Jakarta for two years," is in for some heated debate, especially if he has promised to go back to the office the next day with a decision.

Interests: Interests are an important issue. All work and no play is, for most, a bad thing. You need to look at your interests and hobbies alongside the job and your future career intentions. Can they move forward together? How much time do you want to put into both hobbies and work? These are not easy questions and must be worked out over a period of time. Even so there may come times when there are clashes. If you have thought it all through and discussed it with other family members as appropriate then transient problems are more likely to be just that – transient.

There are no right or wrong answers here and I would not presume to give advice. The amount of time and energy a job needs to take up and what must be left for other things varies between individuals and rightly so; otherwise it would be a dull old world if we were all the same. The smooth planning of these issues certainly helps you make career decisions more easily and more promptly than would otherwise be the case. And for most, success in life means career and private life working reasonably compatibly together, whatever the demands of the job at any particular moment.

All this information forms the basis for much of the subsequent thinking that is necessary as you consider how you may take action through the way you work and what you think and do so as to build your career successfully. Opportunities and your real circumstances constantly have to be compared. Some career paths will play to your strengths, others will not and some will cause a clash of objectives that will be problematical or will simply not be open to you because of your mix of talents and abilities (though this latter is something you can work at correcting). The picture you build up here is solely for *your own* benefit. Some of the facts and information may also be useful at appraisals and in the documentation and discussion that may be necessary if you wish to change employer (of which more later).

OBTAIN PROFESSIONAL CAREER GUIDANCE

Sometimes, the problem appears that as you try to analyse both yourself and the path you want to take, you can come to no real conclusion as to what will suit you best in the future. In this case, it may be worth seeking professional assistance. An example of such a circumstance may make a point clearer.

I came from a background that had no links with the commercial or business world. My father was in the medical profession and once he had got over the shock of my wanting to go into "industry", insisted that I should first go to an organisation called the Vocational Guidance Association. This body undertook to test the aptitudes of a person and match them to the type of job and career that seem most suited to the individual concerned. As my father was paying, I agreed to go, and found myself subjected to a battery of psychometric tests that lasted most of a day. A report cataloguing what little ability I had at that stage arrived a few days later.

To cut a long story short, I did go into industry (publishing) and cannot now remember what difference, if any, the report made. What I do remember is finding it many years later when I moved house. It described the nature of the job they had felt I would most enjoy, and I found it matched *exactly* those things which I was involved in at that time. I have always had a greater respect for such services since. An objective view is sometimes useful, and while there is no test that will magically put you into a career you love and excel in, such analysis can provide may be very useful.

Such services are available in most large cities and can be useful at many stages of a career. They are by no means only designed for those moving from education to a first job. Choose a good advisor (not everyone who offers such testing is good) and this may be for some a useful check at a particular stage of their career.

MATCH YOUR ANALYSIS OF YOURSELF WITH MARKET DEMANDS

Whatever picture your various self-analysis exercises build up, it must be match realistically with the demands made by employers in the marketplace. Let me put that more specifically: it must match up with the demands made by employers in the section of industry and commerce in which you intend to excel. So, whilst there are perhaps generally desirable characteristics that we might list: being adaptable to change (or able to prompt it), flexible, or thorough or productive and so on, there will be more specific characteristics in terms of abilities and nature which will be demanded in a particular field. Indeed, a certain characteristic may be an asset in one area and frowned on in another, as something like creativity might be differently regarded in an advertising agency and a more traditional business. Similarly, what for some is drive and initiative, others will regard as aggressive and self-seeking.

Two points arise from this. First, having analysed yourself and your intended field (even if you are already in it), you must aim to cultivate the profile for success in that field. Or, for some, react to such analysis showing that all the signs are that you are not well suited in a way that encourages the possibility of success in a particular area. The better the match, the better the chances that your profile will allow you to do well, and progress along your chosen path.

But a good match is not, of itself, sufficient, as I said there is a second point here, illustrated by an anecdote: a good friend has a son who has just left acting college and is intent on carving out a career on the stage. I went to see a play he was in at a small London "fringe" theatre; a production in which the cast were all young people starting out on their careers. His performance seemed to me excellent, and I said as much to my friend later. "What else did you notice?" He asked and, when I could not think what he meant, he commented, "The whole of the cast was excellent." His point was that talent was not going to be the only factor in his son's success if it comes, he has to get ahead of a strong field to rise to the rank of star. So it is in many fields. Just having the right qualifications and aptitudes is rarely sufficient – others have them too – you have to have them in the right amount and at the right level; and they must show. Then, with some luck and if you work at it, you may carve out success for yourself. But never make the mistake of thinking this happens in a vacuum – it happens with others around you trying to do similar things. Knowing how well you match up is, nevertheless, a good starting point – one worth some thought.

SUM UP YOUR ANALYSIS IN CLEAR OBJECTIVES

Every management guru has their own version of the maxim that every business must have a plan or, as it is sometimes put, "if you do not know there you are going, any road will do". It is true, it does make a difference; as with any business, so with any career. This really is common sense, and yet conversely it is so very easy to wake up one day and find that what we have been wont to regard as planning is bowing to the inevitable and, if it looks good, taking the credit for it. Having said that objectives are important, another point should be made: they must be flexible. Life in all its aspects, certainly in business, is dynamic.

Objectives cannot be allowed to act as a straightjacket, yet we need their guidance, so their potential for acting to fix things should not be regarded as a reason not to have them.

In business, people talk of "rolling" plans: a plan that is reasonably clear and comprehensive for the shorter term, then sets out broad guidelines and further ahead has only main elements clearly stated. As time rolls by, the plan can be updated and advanced into the future. With your career in mind, you will find a similar approach works well. In the short term, when you can anticipate more of what may happen, the detail of how you intend to proceed is clearer; further ahead you have notes on the outline strategy and key issues.

Remembering to say "My objective is to become a marketing director" is not much help without some clear actions and steps along the way. Objectives should be SMART. This well-known mnemonic stands for specific, measurable, achievable, realistic and timed, thus:

- **Specific** – expressed clearly and precisely
- **Measurable** – it must be possible to tell if you have achieved it (the difference between saying you want to be "very successful" or "marketing director")
- **Achievable** – it must not be so difficult as to be pie in the sky, otherwise the plan that goes with it similarly becomes invalid and of no practical help in taking things forward
- **Realistic** – it must fit with your self-analysis and be what you want; it might be a valid objective to aim for

something possible but not ideal (promotion might be possible within a department, but your real intention is to get out beyond that) but this will not be helpful. Action is needed with more ambitious objectives in mind

- **Timed** – this is important, objectives are not to be achieved "eventually" but by a particular moment: when do you aim to be marketing director? – This year, next year or when?

There is no need for elaborate documentation here. Any objectives and plans are purely for your own guidance, but a few notes on paper may be useful and there are times (such as appraisal or when training is contemplated) when it may be useful to think of current events alongside the notes you have made. If you not only know which road you should be on, but have taken steps to make sure you go purposively along it, that is a good start.

CHAPTER 3
PEOPLE POWER

THOSE THAT HELP OR HINDER

Take the people out of business and there is little left. People issues show themselves in many ways and there is an overlap here between this and communication, dealt with in its own sections. Career development is an interactive process; it is not something you can do in isolation. Here we review a number of people factors that, whether simple or more complex, must not be forgotten and can assist practically with making your career development activity successful.

KEEP A PEOPLE FILE

Problems, opportunities and people go together. So often when something crops up and you need information, assistance or advice, the first thought that comes to mind is related to a person: "They'll know," you say to yourself, and then you think again. You can see them in your mind's eye. You know you met them at that conference you attended in Penang, or was it Hong Kong? You had a meal together, you... but what was their name? What company did they work for? Where is their business card? You cannot find the name and something that might be sorted in two minutes on the telephone ends up taking an hour. We all do it.

In some ways, no great harm is done. After all, you cannot keep in touch with everyone and it is difficult to know who will be useful in five years' time (remember career development is a long term process). But it is probably better to note too many names than to miss good ones. Therefore, you need a people file. This is a little more than an address book or a file for business cards. It needs to record some information about each person, enough so that you can call something to mind about them. For instance, record:

- The date you met
- Where you met
- The circumstances of meeting (did you sit next to them on a flight or meet them at a conference?)
- Also: were you introduced by a third party (and if so, who that person was) and keep name, position, company, contact details, etc. and also maybe something about them ("knows all about regression analysis" or "can recommend a good restaurant in Tokyo").

There can be no half measures here. It must be done systematically, it must be done regularly (it is amazing how quickly some of the detail about someone is forgotten) and it must include everyone that may be useful in the future. You can always prune it a little over the months and years so that it remains manageable. There is an old saying that "it is not what you know, but who you know" that matters in life. If there is any truth in this (and there must be) you have to know who you know. Such a system is not an option in career development, it is a prerequisite.

USE NETWORKING

Before we networked, we kept in touch. It is no good having a good network of contacts, safely noted (as just mentioned) and then not keeping them "live". You have to keep in touch.

It matters less how this is done than that it should happen. The frequency will vary amongst your list of contacts, some only need a card once a year, at Christmas or New Year perhaps, others need to be called a couple of times every month. And some will contribute to the frequency of contact by contacting you; networking is a two-way street.

Sometimes the contact is social, sometimes it is based on a specific request for help and information, sometimes it is unashamed brain-picking.

Before he retired, I used to see an American consultant regularly. He would phone up and say he was in town and suggest a lunch or breakfast. He was a nice guy and it was always good to see him. It was also enormously stimulating. He could pack more ideas, more creative thinking and more examples to back up points made into what was essentially a social contact than anyone I have ever met. An hour and a half with him was like a mini seminar and it was tiring, you did not realise how much you were thinking and concentrating until you came away from the session. I learnt a great deal from him, but he did too; he was an unashamed brain-picker of the highest order. Good networking is like this. It is interesting, it is fun, and yet we learn from it and thus keeping up with people can be a constructive process.

The only down side is that it is time consuming and you have to balance the need to keep your contacts live with the other time pressures in your job and life. One thing is sure, the old principle of two heads being better than one can work well, so this activity can pay dividends - speaking for myself I have received three unsolicited job offers from such contacts over my career, and I accepted two of them!

MIX IN THE RIGHT CIRCLES

The last two sections have commented on who you know, keeping a note of them and keeping in touch. Now we turn to how you get to know them in the first place, or at least some of them. You need to work at cultivating contacts. Just where and how this is done will depend on the nature of your job and the kind of business you are in, but some general principles apply.

Internally you need to take an interest in the organisation at large – who does what, who runs what and knows what. Most organisations have an informal communications network as important as the formal structure, and this just means that in a large organisation there is quite a bit of ground to cover. On the basis that you only get out of something what you put in, it is worth seeking opportunities to contribute in ways that mix you with the right people. What committees, working parties and project teams should you be on? Some will be very useful, putting you in touch with the prime movers and giving you an opportunity to demonstrate your competence. Others are a waste of time and what is more if you get a reputation for being perpetually on such groups it will not do your credibility any good at all. Some will be contentious and you may have to consider the wisdom of being part of the team that moved the office from its prestigious quarters into what many regard as a slum on some distant industrial estate, even if it did save a great deal of money. You can no doubt think of other examples. Such well-chosen activity is sensible and useful.

Externally, the same kind of thinking applies. For example, what should you belong to and participate in – the local management institute, trade, professional and technical bodies, and other interest groups, clubs? There may be sense in something from all or some of these categories. Again pick carefully, get involved where this is more useful than simply belonging and turning up at meetings, and work out an order of priorities as you are unlikely to be able to do everything.

The moral here is that just sitting in your office, even if you are doing an excellent job, does not give you such a high profile as operating and being seen to operate across a wider canvass. When opportunities come up, perhaps in discussion, amongst a group of senior managers, you want your credentials to come readily to mind, it helps to be in those minds, preferably filed in a number of different places. The first necessity, before any such opportunity is likely to be aimed your way, is quite simple – to be remembered.

RECRUIT A MENTOR

One of the motivations for a manager, or at least for some managers, is the satisfaction of helping people develop and of seeing them do well. I was, looking back, very lucky in that two of the people I worked for early in my career were like this. I learned a great deal form both and learned it very much quicker than would otherwise have been the case. I am not, on the other hand, at all sure that if I had not this luck I would have had the wits to seek out such assistance; my career planning was too naïve in those days.

The ideal mentor is sufficiently senior to have knowledge, experience and clout. They need the process to appeal to them, and they need to have time to put into the process; this need not be great, the key thing is to have the willingness to spend some time regularly helping someone else. If your boss and your mentor is one and the same person, that might be ideal, but it is not essential. Usually, if such a relationship lasts, it will start out one way – they help you – and become more two-way over the years; perhaps the person on the mentor side makes the decision to help rather on the basis of this anticipated possibility.

After the first few years of a career, there is no reason why you cannot have regular contact with a number of people where in each case the relationship is of this nature. This can take various forms. In my own case, for instance, my work in marketing overlaps sometimes with the area of market research. While I know a good deal about aspects of this, certainly in terms of what can be done with it, I have no real strength in the techniques involved. But I have a research mentor. Someone who can help and advise me in this particular field. This is very useful and works on the basis of a swap, in other words he helps in that way and I am able (I hope) to advise and assist him in other ways. This is a not uncommon basis.

This kind of thing should be regarded as really very different from, and very much more than, networking. The nature and depth of the interaction and the time and regularity of it is much more extensive. This is not primarily a career assistance process in the sense of someone who will give you a leg up the organisation through recommendation or lobbying, though this can of course occur. It is more important in helping develop the range and depth of your competences and this in turn acts to boost your career.

HELP OTHERS (AND REMEMBER TO SAY THANK YOU)

There is a danger that some of the suggestions of this section, keeping a people file, networking, etc. may seem somewhat soulless and one-sided. This is not so and what you can achieve in these ways will be minimised if you see it like that. The simplest way of injecting a two-way element into these dealings is to remember to thank those who offer assistance whether it is advice or something more tangible. First, this is just common courtesy, it is appreciated and makes it more likely that those others involved will be disposed to help you again. A written note is often more appropriate than simply a word, especially when directed at the older generation.

Secondly, this kind of assistance is a two-way street. You will be more able to obtain the further assistance you need if you return any favours, indeed not only is it useful to have the reputation for being a ready source of assistance for others, the whole process actually becomes more interesting and satisfying. In busy life it is all too easy to lose touch, not get back to people or otherwise put good networking relationships at risk. Sit back and think – who do you owe a thank you to?

Two further topics fit here and are worth a word, first:

OFFICE POLITICS

Unless your office is the exception, it may be that you have noticed that in others, whilst on the surface they run smoothly, efficiently and with hardly a murmur to interrupt the air of pleasant calm, there can be something of an underlying hint of intrigue. In others again, there is an unconcealed hotbed of rivalry, enmity and backbiting. If you were to find yourself in such an environment you would doubtless stand back from it, stay neutral and uninvolved, and get on with the job. And if you find a single person who believes that, then take immediate steps to sell them London's Tower Bridge; their gullibility must be immense. Office politics too deserves a mention here under the People heading.

Even if you did stand back from it all, would you thrive? The trouble with being in the middle of the road is the pronounced tendency to get run over. And the least said about what sitting on the fence does to you the better.

In most organisations some degree of office politics is one of the givens. Indeed, it is normal and perhaps, given human nature, inevitable. But what does this mean exactly? On the one hand it conjures up a picture of jockeying for a place on the Board, fighting to become Head of Department, or plotting to take over as CEO. On the other hand, office politics includes a level of activity at which the goal is seeing who can get the most praise, the largest salary increase, the best office, the most up to date mobile phone or just the seat nearest the window. What is more, and make no mistake about this, the most vicious infighting is often over the comparatively small prizes. Hell hath no fury like those who feel that they have unjustly been denied the key to the Executive Washroom. This is, after all, not something you can forget, and indeed you will doubtless be reminded of it several times a day as you go about your ablutions.

These undercurrents show themselves in a hundred and one different ways each day. They show in conversation. In the insults – *There are only two things I don't like about you – your face*; in the rumours – *I hear that what's his name in Research is for the chop*; in a dozen different phrases that are designed, not to help, but to stir things up in some way. They show in the manoeuvring for position, in the bluff and double bluff, in the way that even the mildest mannered employee can be roused to fury by the feeling that they have been slighted, and in the way in which even the most well positioned individuals still seem to strive for more. Everyone seems to be after something; whether it is control of the whole organisation or just a new filing cabinet... And whether you get what you want or not, be your ambition large or small, does matter; at least it does to you.

So, realistically, office politics is something that involves everybody to some degree – whether initially they admit it or not. The question is, therefore, what do you do about it? How involved do you get and what do you have to watch for, watch out for and do? There is of course no single neat answer. There is no one thing you can do that will whisk you to the top of the organisational hierarchy, certainly no magical gesture like snapping your fingers and shouting, *Promotion!* Like so much in organisational life, achieving success is bereft of magic formulae. There are, however, a variety of aspects of office life through which you can exert some positive influence, or use to watch your back.

Winning the workplace battle is not, to say the least, an exact science. Without care, planning and guile you are left subject to circumstances and other peoples' ambition.

There are only two overall ways of setting out to win the office war. If you are to progress unscathed through the office jungle, indeed if you are not just to survive but to prosper, one approach is just to do a good job, trusting that the powers that be will notice what you do, and that virtue will bring its own reward. You may believe this is sufficient. You may be right: good work and a measure of good luck may conceivably be enough. Pigs might fly; there is evidence aplenty that just doing a good job does *not* automatically always get the recognition it deserves, and certainly looking like a doormat pretty much guarantees to get you trodden on. As for good luck, that can only ever be certainly relied upon to explain the success of your rivals.

Alternatively, you can do both a good job and work at ensuring that people – the right people – do notice. So that you do get the recognition you deserve and achieve some of your other goals along the way, the latter approach may be a safer bet. Working on being a success is even more important if you are not in fact doing a good job; which is exactly what some of those who thrive in business do. So, you must be careful about everything from the profile you project and the accuracy and style of your communications to the people you meet along the way; they could be friend or foe and it is worth remembering a phrase attributed to Ashleigh Brilliant, *"I always win. You always lose. What could be fairer than that?"*

Careers need managing and realistically one thread of this is to avoid the negative side of office politics and use those things that will assist your security and progress. Certainly it is another area where success does not just happen – it needs working at and it needs care; a ruthless political approach may draw sanctions, ignoring the whole thing can see you disadvantaged.

Finally, though this will not necessarily apply to everyone, a topic that, despite that, has lessons for us all.

A MANAGEMENT ROLE

While we are considering people it is worth mentioning management. A common route ahead in many organisations involves acquiring a role in which you supervise other people. Fine you may say, I'll become a manager. No reason why not perhaps, but let me digress for a moment. Before going on it is worth linking progress into management with other possible routes ahead. In many fields, and in many organisations, progress within the organisation, including the rewards that can accompany it, is inherently linked to a management role. Thus:

- Success at one thing leads to promotion into a *different* role
- Some of the skills that made you successful in the past may *not* help you as a manager
- Additional skills demanded by management may *not* play to your strengths
- The job of managing people may, or may not, be something you enjoy of itself rather than wanting because it takes you up the organisation hierarchy

Thus you may need to pause, reflect and consider – do you *really want to be a manager?* If not, and it is something that you might not only not enjoy but which you might not be good at, you may need to consider other ways ahead.

If it is for you then you need to be aware that management is a unique process with its own demands in terms of approaches that make it work; let's define it in more detail:

Being a manager involves people; other people. You may still have work of your own to do, but additionally you have others reporting to you. At its simplest, management is:

- Achieving results *through* other people, and
- Usually doing so towards specific, tangible, often financial, objectives.
- Management is more than work allocation - deciding who does what. It is *not* just doing things *for* other people – and the process of management takes, time,

41

effort and expertise. Of these the one most easily underestimated is time. You still almost certainly have your own tasks to do – the executive part of the job so to speak – but you must create adequate time to manage those reporting to you.

SO WHAT DOES MANAGEMENT INVOLVE?

Let's look at the tasks and skills involved. Once you have people reporting to you, the classic six tasks involved in managing them are:

1. Planning (what must be done to achieve the desired results)
2. Organising (time, people and activities)
3. Recruitment and selection (to create or replenish the team)
4. Training and development (to keep peoples' skills sharp)
5. Motivation (creating and maintaining positive attitudes amongst the team)
6. Control (monitoring performance standards and taking any necessary action in the light of results).

And the overall orchestration of everything: all this, and whatever work the team does, implies. If that seems a lot then, yes, it needs some juggling. You are going to need to keep a clear head, an eye on both the detail and the broad picture and become expert at the skills the role demands. So the tasks of management demand proficiency in a number of skills. These will vary depending on the exact nature of the job you do, but are likely to include:

- Decision making and problem solving
- Time management
- A variety of communications skills (business writing,

making formal presentations, running meetings, one to one liaison with staff, interviewing etc.).

Whatever else a management role involves, it is the manager's responsibility to create a vision. This may sound intangible, but it is not. It links closely with having clear objectives, and it goes further. You need to provide:

- Clarity of purpose
- A belief that delivering excellence is necessary, worthwhile and possible
- A feeling of interest (better still excitement) about achieving goals
- A link between the overall picture and the needs and satisfactions of the individual members of the team.

All this can focus corporately or, more likely early on, on section or department.

The full range of management techniques is clearly beyond our brief here. But two things should be noted: first management is a specific role demanding specific skills – and is not for everyone. Secondly, while it is certainly progress for some to move into management, thriving in that position and moving on up that hierarchy is dependent on being a good manager.

CHAPTER 4
THE POWER OF
COMMUNICATION

MAKING IT WORK, MAKING IT USEFUL

Most of what goes on in business is, in fact, communications; and anything that is not is probably dependent on some form of communications to initiate it or keep it going. If you are in business then you are in communications. Your ability to communicate and the way in which you do so is so important to your career that here it is dealt with under its own heading, though it is certainly one of a number of career management skills which are dealt with elsewhere.

RECOGNISE THE DIFFICULTIES OF COMMUNICATION

The first step to using good communications to further your career is to recognise the difficulties and resolve to work at avoiding them; more than that to resolve to excel at communications.

As a busy person you communicate all the time – verbally, in writing, with a variety of people – and do so perfectly well most of the time. Occasionally, however, you will find someone asking, "What do you mean?" in response to something which you have said. Sometimes you initiate the correction – "But I meant." and sometimes people will say to you: "You want me to do *what*?" As you can see, communication is not always as easy as it seems. All this may simply cause a bit of confusion, and take a moment to sort out, but it can cause major problems either immediately or later.

If you are going to work with people and you are going to get things done you need to communicate clearly and, very often, persuasively. What is more you need to be seen to do so. Your communication breakdowns can cause problems for others, something that is hardly likely to mark you out as a high flyer. Your communications successes label you as competent, capable and on occasion mark your abilities as excellent. They are disproportionately important because, as we shall see, excellence in communication may well be read by others as indicating a broader competence. And the need to persuade, getting your own way, particularly being able to obtain support for decisions and action that prove successful, is simply vital. Few careers progress without a strength in this area. The next sections examine the most important aspects of this fact.

COMMUNICATE CLEARLY

Crystal clarity should be the aim of all your communication. (It goes without saying, at least in this section, that if you are going to communicate you have to have something worthwhile to say – assuming that, whatever it is must be made clear.) The last section highlighted the inherent difficulty of successful communication. Here I want to help you think about making it clear and surmounting those difficulties. As luck would have it, prevailing standards are on your side because every office in the world tends to be witness to regular communications breakdown. Habit and prevailing style can compound the problem with "office gobbledygook", bureaucracy, jargon and complexity dressed up as substance all combining to obscure any meaning that may lurk within the confusion.

You can probably think of examples in your own office,

at meetings, in memos, or just in conversation over coffee where you come away saying: "What was all that about?"

As a result, things are delayed, communication takes up more time than it should and, at worst, mistakes are made and things go wrong. The career-minded can simply not afford to be like this, because the other thing that happens is that individuals are linked to and characterised by their communication style. If you are clear, really clear, then you stand out in this sea of confusion, and do so to your advantage.

Think of the impact of clarity; a clear succinct summary in a report or proposal, a complex sequence of events spelt out so that the key elements shine forth, a plan, policy or procedure that all can understand first time - these are all noticeable to their recipients. Such things stand out because they make understanding easy for those to whom the communication is directed. If you can do this and do it consistently in your job, and get a reputation for so doing, it creates a powerful feeling of confidence in your abilities. A poor plan well explained is not as good as a good plan well explained, but both are likely to do better than a poor plan poorly explained.

LISTEN (REALLY LISTEN)

Communication is a two-way street. It is important how you put any message over but it is also important how you respond. One key response to other peoples' communication is to listen. It is always a compliment to be described as a "good listener".

Listening, and being prepared to listen, makes an impression. And, of course, there is the immediate feedback that will help you to manage any conversation better. But there is listening, and there is listening. The trouble is that the mind can listen faster than people can speak - yes, literally. This means that the mind has time to wander as you listen (often getting ready what you are going to say next, especially if it is contradictory) and it does just that; so, listening becomes inefficient. The result? The all too frequent: "Sorry, what did you say?" which can signal not simply inattention, but lack of interest, and this alone is sufficient to begin to get two people at cross purposes.

Listening is vital. You must resolve to be a good listener; an *active* listener. The result is worth striving for as really listening gives you the edge in conversation and labels you as a sensitive communicator. And, as has been said, everything that builds your ability to be, and be seen to be a good communicator, is valuable in career terms.

SEEK AND WATCH FOR FEEDBACK

Listening, referred to above, is only one, albeit major, form of feedback in communication. You will only be a good communicator if you resolve to note and use all the signs given by others and work at doing so. This implies a number of things. That you should:

*   Watch for visible signs (gestures, expressions, etc.)
*   Listen for non-verbal signs (things not said but sounded, such as a grunt of disapproval or a tut of impatience)
*   Ask questions (itself a skill worth cultivating)
*   Read between the lines – in speech as well as in writing – to see what may be really meant. As I am sure you have noticed people do not always say what they mean; thus a sentence that begins, "With the greatest respect..." is usually followed by an argument that respects the other party very little if at all.

All this and more will put you in a better position to communicate more effectively (and more efficiently, because it will keep matters on tract). Again it is a skill to be cultivated, part of the comprehensive overall ability you need as a communicator if you are to use this ability as a skill to further your career.

So far in this section on communications, the points have

been about communications generally. This is important enough, but there are several aspects, or particular forms of communication, which are especially important to the effectiveness of an individual in an organisational environment, and thus to their career prospects. We turn to these in the next few sections.

YOU MUST BE ABLE TO PRESENT FORMALLY

There is an old saying which runs: "The human brain is a wonderful thing. It starts working on the day you are born, goes on and on and never stops until the day you must stand up and speak in public." You may know the feeling, indeed even the most experienced presenter may experience things like a dry mouth, shaking hands, "butterflies in the stomach" to make this a traumatic experience.

Quite recently, a firm approached me as a consultant. They had both a complex organisation and a complex pattern of obtaining business which involved formal presentations as one of the key stages. Some of their technical people were poor at this and I was asked to suggest as to how to arrange matters so that the technical people did not have to undertake presentations.

Wrong question – their customers wanted to reassure themselves about the technical viability of their products and services – they wanted to hear what the technical people had to say. The answer then had to be to equip them to do the presentational task better. There are so many circumstances in which the skills of formal presentation are needed in, for example:

- Presenting to customers
- Dealings with suppliers and collaborators
- Internally
- Negotiations with banks, accountants, shareholders, etc.

There are a hundred and one different ways where plans, ideas or developments are dependent on how something is put over and it must be put over "on your feet". It is for most, if not all, people *simply not something you can avoid*. There can be only one response from anyone intent on career development: you have to learn to present and learn to do it well.

If you are not currently comfortable with this area, do not despair. It is a skill and can be learnt (I know, it an area where I do a great deal of training and I have seen many people over the years amaze themselves with just what they can do – once they know how to go about it). What makes it easier? Preparation is the first thing, a clear structure – a beginning, a middle and an end – is important, and there are a variety of tricks of the trade that will assist. A complete run down on what makes for success is beyond the brief for this book. But make no mistake: people tend not to say what an excellent plan, what a pity it was not better presented, they say what a bad presentation, it cannot be much of a plan – and the same principle is applied to the presenter. Thus a good presenter is not only more likely to get approval for whatever is presented, they are in all likelihood going to be seen as a step or two up in terms of overall personal competence than someone weak in this area. You may feel this is an area to investigate: not for nothing has the phrase "death by PowerPoint" gone into the language and poor practice gets copied as the norm leading, at best, to the bland leading the bland.

The best way to improve these skills, having investigated them, is practice. It may well be that if you want to add the power of presentation to those skills that will help your career, you should actively seek out opportunities to make some. Providing you think about it, the more you present, the more your technique for doing it will improve. Not only is it useful, there is a great deal of satisfaction to be had from a presentation that is well executed and well received.

"Writing is easy; all you do is sit staring at a blank sheet of paper until the drops of blood form on your forehead." This was said (by Gene Fowler) about creative writing, but is might come equally to mind as you contemplate that report you have to submit to the Board in two days' time. The message in this section is similar to that contained in the section above on formal presentations. Most jobs come with paperwork – some of this is routine administration, some is very important.

Just like presentations, written communication, reports, proposals, even minutes and memos, can have a great deal hanging on them. Decisions that you want to go a particular way may be influenced not only by the quality of the thought, idea or proposal but by how the case for it is made and how well it is expressed in writing. Consider a report. Think of one you have had to read. If it is clear, well-structured, descriptive; if it had a clear introduction and a succinct summary that really ties together the key issues, then it makes much more impact on you – and it says something about the writer. Any report speaks volumes about the skill, knowledge, expertise, competence of the writer – and their clout. Yours must do the same.

Again, this is a skill that can be developed. In my own case, my career took a path that made certain kinds of writing very important, first with proposals and reports when I first went into consultancy, then later with books. Not only is there often much hanging on these things, but they have a permanence that, say, a presentation does not. They stay around to haunt you and bosses are quite capable of producing for discussion at an appraisal meeting, a copy of a report written nine months or more previously.

So this too is also a skill worth investigating (another book in this series is *Smart skills: Business* Writing) and one that you can spend a lifetime fine-tuning. So it should be with your business writing – regular work on it will improve it.

And an effective and appropriate style will reflect well on you in your current job and in the view taken by others regarding your future.

A last point may provide an added incentive for you to work on your skills in this area. As your writing ability improves, you will also find you get to do it faster. This saves time and is a worthwhile objective in its own right. You have only to look at the quality of much of the paperwork that circulates around many an office to see that prevailing standards often leave something to be desired; so write right and you have another essential skill that can make you stand out.

YOUR COMMUNICATION MUST BE PERSUASIVE

With much business communication, it is not enough to be clear and prompt understanding; there is a need to persuade. People with whom you must communicate up, down and around the organisation are not going to agree with you instantly and automatically just because you communicate well. They have their own point of view and this may include not doing anything or doing something quite different from what you are suggesting. Selling is part of many jobs. It may not be called that, or even thought of as that, but that is what it is, any other word is perhaps a euphemism.

Now you may feel instinctively that you are not a salesperson and that this is something that you really do not need to be involved in to do your job. You may be right; but how about this: would you like to get your own way more often? Would you like less argument about things? Would you like to be seen more as a leader and initiator, someone who makes things happen rather than just follows? If the answer to any of these points is affirmative then you need to be able to communicate persuasively. If I am doing this it is, in part, because I am putting up a case for doing so on the basis that it will help *you*. If I just said do it, I think it is right, then this is less powerful. Selling – persuasive communication – demands an approach based on an understanding of the people or person to be persuaded, something that sounds pretty much common sense, but it is also something where common sense and the various techniques involved needs coordinating and thus needs investigating and learning before it can be successfully deployed. However you do it, there will be many occasions in your career where your progress will benefit from being able to communicate persuasively. Agreed?

YOU MUST BE AN EFFECTIVE NEGOTIATOR

This is another communication skill with a direct link to both effectiveness and your career. Negotiation overlaps with persuasiveness. It is to do not just with whether an idea will be accepted or agreed – that is the job of selling – but *how* agreement will be arranged, what the terms and conditions are to be. Again there are so many applications internally and externally to the organisation, again it is a body of knowledge and techniques skillfully deployed that make it possible, again it is something worth investigation and practice. The balance of arrangements that negotiation can settle is important to activities all the way up the management hierarchy, if you start as you mean to go on and become adept in this regard it will stand you in good stead.

MEET WITH CONFIDENCE – AS A PARTICIPANT

It would be wrong to omit something about meetings in this section. Much communication within the workplace is not one to one but involves the interactions of groups - the ubiquitous meeting. Sometimes it seems to most of us that we spend far too long in meetings that achieve far too little, a situation that gives rise to remarks such as: "the ideal meeting is two – with one absent". On the other hand, whatever the topic of the meeting, those attending it are on show, especially if representatives of senior management are present. If, when called on to contribute, you are unprepared, tongue tied, incoherent or muddled and indecisive then you not only fail to; make whatever point you wanted to make, you are visibly tagged with an "indecisive" label, or whatever label seems appropriate to your performance.

So, if you are at a meeting (make sure incidentally that you should be; you do not want to be seen attending what others regard as time-wasting sessions that hamper your productivity; particularly if they *are* time-wasting), go prepared. Always read the last minutes, and any notes or papers circulated for discussion, in advance. No matter that others may not; you should. There will be issues that face you that you can only pronounce on with some thought beforehand and you cannot afford to be caught out for the sake of a moment's "homework".

Be careful not to come over as showing off, but remember the key points of effective meeting participation:

- Be prepared
- Listen
- Make notes
- Keep comments succinct and to the point
- Deal through the Chair and respect the agenda and any meeting formalities
- Do not be crowded out, if you have a point to make, ensure you do so
- Never resort to abuse, but be prepared to fight your corner on a rational businesslike basis to make your point
- Be open-minded and respect others' points of view (though you do not have to agree with them).

Politeness coupled with firmness, assertiveness rather than aggression – all these make for a good meeting. If you can become known as someone who brings common sense, sound thinking and appropriate manner to a meeting, you will get asked to the right ones more often and your performance at them will contribute to your being seen in the right light. Never become unthinking in even a routine meeting – you are always on show and there may well always be something to gain from them.

MEET WITH CONFIDENCE – CHAIRING THE SESSION

You may well have noticed that however well or badly a meeting goes, its manner is usually a direct reflection of the manner of the chairperson and, if no one is in the chair, the thing is usually a muddle from beginning to end. You are not going to rise any great distance up most organisations without the ability not only to attend a meeting and perform impressively, but also to chair one.

For the CEO at least, their position and authority will work in their favour to keep things going well in some respects. Down the line, it is perfectly possible to find yourself chairing a meeting where some of those attending are more senior and more experienced than you. So it is an area where, though practice of course helps, you have to make a good start. Therefore, it is another skill worth researching. The chairperson must:

- Be prepared (preferably more thoroughly prepared than others attending)
- Set and keep to the agenda and keep time (an ability to run to time is especially impressive to others)
- keep control, yet encourage discussion, let people have their say and comply with any rules
- Be able to field questions, arbitrate in debate and referee in argument
- See, and deal with, both sides of the case
- Summarise clearly
- Arbitrate where necessary
- Prompt and record decisions and maintain a reasonable consensus.

And more, no doubt. This is another communication skill that will stand you in good stead in a number of fields and circumstance. Resolve to be a good chairman, acquire the skills to be so and use them fairly as chairmanship is not about riding roughshod over everyone by sheer weight. Apart from anything else, the roughshod approach will be resented by others. Get things done, but get people feeling they are good decisions sensibly arrived at and that they contributed to the process and they will be queuing up to attend your meetings!

ASK QUESTIONS

There is a danger that we think about communications as concerned only with how we communicate to pass information or instructions to others. But the ability to thrive and do your job successfully is dependent on knowledge and information and all you need of this will not be delivered on a plate. You have to ask. Sometimes you have to balance this with not becoming a nuisance to those you ask, but otherwise the rule is ask, ask and ask some more. This should become a habit. Its value is cumulative and the effect is most often useful and the impression positive. Open questions (those that cannot be answered "yes" or "no") tend to work best at unearthing the most information promptly and easily.

Having asked, of course you must listen and note anything you need to retain. Communication is two-way and abilities in all the specialist areas of communication dealt with here not only highlight the general importance, but also pick methodologies that are prime candidates for career enhancement. It really cannot be stated too strongly: if your communications skills are weak then your career prospects can all too easily be restricted. Even in technical areas where you may feel other specialist skills make up for deficiencies here, they may not be able to be hidden. So give attention to the way in which you communicate and make sure you do it in a way that benefits you.

Imagine someone calls you out of the blue. You have not seen them for a while and you invite them for a meal. You are pleased to see them, you lay on the arrangements rather specially and a very good evening results. Then a few days later, you get either a telephone call to say thank you or a specially written note. Which would make the best impression as a "thank you"? Even in this digital age most people would probably think that the letter was extra nice, taking more trouble than just lifting the telephone. Certainly, whatever view you take, they each make different impressions.

So, any medium of communication has its own special effect. And there are a great many ways of communicating: one to one, a meeting, a memo or letter, an email, a circular or a note on the company bulletin board. They work in different ways. Take email, perhaps the most modern form of universal communication. It speaks of urgency (just like cables and telex did), but it can be less formal - people write in what is almost an internal memo style to contacts in other companies who they have never met and to whom they would be much more formal in a letter. Pick the methodology right and what you do will be thought appropriate; pick wrong and you are thought hasty, uncaring or unthinking. What is the right way to communicate to someone that they are being fired? Or to a group that one member of the team is now in charge? Or to a senior manager so that he is most likely to give time to think about something? Each case and each person needs thought. Getting it right adds something positive to your image.

For some, with both the nerve and the clout to carry it off, a unique style (perhaps graphically) can be added to certain communications. But add this kind of element with care. Getting the method right can add powerfully to what you communicate and what you communicate always says a great deal about you.

JOIN THE GRAPEVINE

The grapevine, or informal communications network, in an organisation may take many forms. In one company in which I worked, it consisted almost entirely of the company tea lady, as she moved round and round the office during the day, so the news – good and bad, accurate and wild rumour – went with her. The tea lady just mentioned was not intent on doing this so much as primed by those who knew how things worked in this respect – anyone aware of the system could have a word with her when the first tea of the day came round in the morning, and know that everyone in the office that day would get the message by the end of the day.

This is not really a digression but it does make a point. Unless you are plugged into the grapevine you may well miss a great deal. Worse, you may put yourself at a disadvantage by not being aware when others are of anything from policy changes to the imminent departure of key members of staff. Of course, you need to be able to read between the lines, not everything the grapevine has to say is true, though even the rumours may have a basis in fact and give you some advance information.

What action does this suggest? First, as I have said, that you should work out how the grapevine works and tap into it. Secondly, you should use it – it is as useful as a channel to pass round what you want to say as it is a source of information. And finally, read, mark and learn from what information it tells you, and use this as part of the image you present of someone well informed, with a finger on the pulse, which can help paint a positive image for you. One caution: if the grapevine is being used politically or maliciously, be very careful; it is one thing to be well informed, it is quite another to be marked down as the instigator of such gossip. That does no one's image any good.

Note: much rumour and gossip moves electronically these days. Think of the problems certain (many?) tweets seem to produce and... be warned.

THINK BEFORE YOU SPEAK

Or as the old saying has it, "engage the brain before the mouth." I suspect that many a career has been blighted by some ill-chosen remark or statement and people left with the feeling that it is all too easy to say something in haste and find yourself repenting at leisure. The consequences of communication may be broad and many. Every time you open your mouth the image of how people see you is adjusted a little and you need to think not just of the context of a comment made but on what other results it may have. In part, this is a matter of manner. It is quite possible to disagree without actually saying "that's rubbish" and, in any case, many matters in business are better for some consideration.

There is rarely a problem in saying "I don't know" or "I would like to think about that" or "Perhaps I could check". Certainly there is less chance of a problem if you go down this road than if you proceed without thought. If this all seems only like so much common sense, so it is. However, before passing on because you feel common sense is your stock in trade, consider for a moment some of the things that can make charging in more likely: anger, surprise, pressure (at being put on the spot), lack of preparation (perhaps prior to a meeting), dislike of the person or proposition with which you are dealing. All make an ill-considered outburst more likely, all make it less likely that such an outburst will match your considered view or be a well-directed piece of communication.

There are moments when biting your tongue and a little thought are great career developers.

CHAPTER 5
CAREER SKILLS

THE USEFUL AND THE NECESSARY

Different jobs need different skills in addition to communications. I do not doubt that a wondrous grasp of the intricacies of regression analysis will help the statistician, almost as an ability to run fast might help a bank robber. However, here I want to review something of skills which have common application in corporate jobs rather than the more specialist skills, though specialist skills – say fluency in a foreign language – may be important to particular circumstances. The following are important in themselves and the attitudes to them discussed may well apply to other areas in your particular field. In the future no doubt, changes, currently difficult to predict, will need adding to such a list. Certainly the rate of change is such these days that in an average career of, say, forty years – age 20 through to 60 (or more) – many things are hardly going to be the same throughout the time spanned.

ACQUIRE A SUITABLE NUMERACY

Mathematics is not everyone's strong suit. But ultimately business is all about profit, and many jobs are involved directly with finance – whether revenue or cost – in one way or another. There are exceptions – non-profit making organisations, charities, government departments and so on, but, while profit may not be the driving force, finance usually plays a key role, so a degree of numeracy is important in very many jobs. Modern management education makes this a less likely gap than in the past. For some, the moral may be to avoid jobs with too much involvement; for others, certainly if you are going in the direction of general management, a certain minimal strength here is essential.

I once heard a tutor on a management course tell a good story to illustrate something in this area. On one particular course, one man could not get anything right in finance and he left the session as very much the class dunce. The group planned to meet up in a year's time to see how everyone was faring, and in due course a dinner was scheduled in a smart hotel. The "dunce" arrived late, but it was clear to all from the Porsche parked in front of the hotel, the suit he wore and a dozen other signs of affluence that he was doing very well for himself. "I would never have thought it possible," said the tutor, "tell us, what are you doing?" "It wasn't easy," he replied, "I tried various things, but I finally ended up in the import/export business in Africa. I discovered that I could buy goods on one side of the border for $2 and sell them on the other for $4. It's just amazing how that 2 per cent adds up." The more numerate reader will recognise that this is not at all how percentages work, and for most of us such a gap in our expertise is unlikely to work out so well.

BE COMPUTER LITERATE

For some, computer literacy is already the norm. Others are currently either struggling or moving closer to some expertise in this area, a process which will never end as the technology moves on inexorably all the time.

The so-called "IT revolution" (information technology) is having a wide effect on many different aspects of business, not only within an organisation, but in terms of communication between organisations and with groups such as suppliers and customers. For example, some salespeople are already carrying and using hand-held tablets to link them to their office, to record information, check stock and input orders. In most stores computerised cash points not only record what has been sold and adjust stock level records, but in some cases the computer involved can automatically reorder more stock direct from a supplier, computer to computer, with no other action involved. One could list a hundred examples, and in a year's time a hundred more.

Most people have to be knowledgeable about what processes can be carried out by computers, many are going to have to work with the various forms of equipment involved and some are going to have to anticipate how all of this will affect their organisations, their people and their commercial prospects. Computers and this kind of technology do not automatically guarantee improvement in every area. There are many things they will not do, some at least they will never do, and some where, although technology has revolutionised the way something is done, it does not guarantee the right end result and in some organisations the statement: "It is in the computer..." has become synonymous with delay or inflexibility. The early computer saying about garbage in and garbage out still applies. For all that, when push comes to shove, there are few people at the time of writing whose careers will not benefit from increasing knowledge and operational ability in this exciting field.

Getting a real grip on whatever forms of technology we all have to use, or will have to use in the future, is important, and some thought within career plans about what you may need is certainly worthwhile.

BE ASSERTIVE

Most if not all organisations are competitive arenas in which to work. It is also a fact of life that excellence in your area of expertise and in your job is not any guarantee of success. In most organisations, there is at least some conflict between departments, activities and individuals.

Now make no mistake, this is not all bad. Friction and competitiveness can act to keep an organisation on its toes, it ensures constant debate and may well have a constructive effect unless it becomes too extreme. In any event it is there. The question is what is the appropriate response to it? The career-minded have, I believe, to adopt an assertive attitude within their work and work environment. There is, it should be noted, all the difference in the world between being assertive and being aggressive. If you are aggressive, and this may well go with – or be seen as going with – being unreasonable, self-seeking, unthinking, selfish and more unflattering descriptions, this is unlikely to do your career good. Though there are people who bludgeon their way to the top through their sheer aggression, this is not so common. Characteristics that better help include being determined and hard-working, having real ambition and pushing for what you want.

Assertiveness is so often necessary in a variety of ways. When you put forward a point of view, a suggestion, or a plan, it must be put over with conviction. If you do seem to present it with all the courage of your convictions, then why should others feel it is demanding of their attention and consideration? Assertiveness is at its most powerful when it is considered. That means to say that while sheer assertiveness will add some credibility to a point of view, if that point is not valid, not well thought out or ill-conceived, then there is no great likelihood of it carrying the day. There is no guarantee that a sound argument will carry the day either, but put over energetically – with some assertion – then it will stand the best chance of acceptance.

This principle must become a habit. Its application would range from one point in a conversation to the preparation of an annual plan or appraisal meeting so that holding back becomes a considered opinion. However, your normal mode of operation and communication, while tailored to the different kinds and levels of people with whom you interact, should always do real justice to the points you wish to make. Successful careers are built on success. You first have to achieve that success before you can benefit from how it positions you within your organisation. Analyse how you come over presently; perhaps you should sometimes consider being just a little more assertive. No, I will restate that – be more assertive where necessary!

MASTER DECISION-MAKING

Decision-making is important in the context of this book in two separate ways. First, the quality of the decisions you make in your job will directly affect your effectiveness and success, and, as is expressed in various ways throughout this book, this, in turn, affects your career. Secondly, you have to make decisions throughout your career about your career and exactly how you can best do this is worth examining in some detail.

To a degree there are no "right" answers in business, but there are certainly wrong ones. Experience is a vital factor in guiding us to pick the right alternative, though too much reliance on it can give a false sense of security and may stifle creativity. A procedure that is logical and systematic and that ensures due consideration of the alternatives, whilst not being infallible, will certainly help make more of your decisions, career or otherwise, turn out right. This leads to what is a neatly ten-step approach:

Step 1: Setting objectives
Before any action can be considered, the objectives of the exercise must be set. Unless you know where you are going, you cannot plan how to get there or how to measure your progress. For the objective to be valuable, it must be as specific and as quantitative as possible. Goals such as "increasing

sales", "improving customer service" and "reducing costs" are useless, as they provide no basis for measurement. If the aim is to increase sales, it should be specified by how much and within what time period.

Step 2: Evaluating the objective against other company objectives
When a clear, precise goal has been established, it should be compared with other company aims to ensure compatibility. Failure to do this is common, particularly in large companies. This results in different sections of the firm working towards objectives which in themselves are reasonable but which when put together become mutually exclusive: for example, the sales office manager may be trying to maintain business with small accounts, whereas marketing or sales management are planning to service them exclusively via wholesalers.

Step 3: Collecting information
Information can now be collected from which plans can be developed. It is unwise to start this data collection stage until clear, compatible objectives have been defined, otherwise vast quantities of useless figures will be assembled "for information" or "in case we need them". The hunger for information has been stimulated by the advance of research techniques and the progressive development of the computer. It is a great temptation to the manager to call for information simply because he knows it is available. Mountains of figures may give a sense of security, but information is costly to process and is only useful (and economic) when it contains answers to precise questions which have direct bearing on the decisions it is possible to take.

Step 4: Analysing the information
It is the objective which will guide you towards the questions to be answered and thus the information needed. The lines of analysis to be followed will in turn be indicated by such

questions. For example, declining sales in one area of the country, perhaps owing to the larger customers buying from competitors, should not prompt us to ask for "everything we know about the market". What we really need is sales in that region broken down by customer type, possibly compared with similar figures for another area. From this analysis, we can proceed progressively through the relevant information, very much more precisely (and probably more quickly and economically) than starting with a dozen different breakdowns that attempt to show "all about everything".

Step 5: Developing alternatives
The whole basis of this method of approach is to encourage you to think more broadly and creatively about possible solutions to problems. Sometimes, of course, the solution will become obvious from systematic processing of the data. In the majority of instances, however, no clear-cut answers will be found, a number of factors suggest themselves, or the answer lies in a combination of a number of factors.

Step 6: Choosing the "best" alternative
This is the heart of the decision-making process. It is unlikely that all possible solutions can be implemented; one must be chosen. To help in this choice, consideration should be made of four criteria: cost, time, risk and resources.

The costs of each alternative can be calculated and compared against the objective. Assuming that several approaches appear to be capable of achieving the objective, this might only narrow the choice. So the other yardsticks should also be used. Time taken might be a critical factor, or the element of risk (particularly of failure) or lack of certain resources might rule out other options: e.g. a critical staff situation in an office may preclude certain courses of action.

The choice of the "best" alternative then is based on a consideration of all the advantages and disadvantages of all the possible alternatives. It is at this stage that experience can be particularly valuable. Its possible limiting effect will already have been overcome by the systematic search for alternatives.

Having made the choice, at least you will be well aware of what you have done in terms of the possible drawbacks of the decision and the discarded alternatives. It will also be easier at some time in the future to look back and assess why such a decision was, in fact, made.

Step 7: Communicating the decision
This is a step too often omitted. And yet unless all concerned know what is being done, impact will be lost. For example, it is commonplace to find inside sales staff whose first knowledge of an advertising campaign is gained from customers. The communication must be systematically planned. Information may well have to be passed by different methods and in different forms to different people, in writing, by telephone, meetings, etc. By communicating only necessary information by the most appropriate methods, far better results will be gained than by a blanket email with copies to everybody.

Step 8: Setting up the control system
Remember that this stage occurs before implementation. This is because in many cases the process of implementing a plan destroys the ability to evaluate it. For example, in a situation where it is believed that inside sales staff lack product knowledge, the decision might be taken to run a training programme. At the end of the course a test is given in which the average score is 90 per cent. It might be concluded, therefore, that the programme was successful. But, as there has been no measurement of what the test score would have been at the beginning of the programme, it can never then be known whether it was successful or not.

Step 9: Implementing the decision
Putting the decision into action should now be easy. It will have been clearly stated what is to be done towards what

objective and why that particular action has been chosen; all concerned will have been informed, and the system of evaluation will have been set. Research has shown that if change is to be implemented, then specific tasks should be allocated to particular people and deadlines laid down for the tasks to be completed. Vague requests for action sometimes, will inevitably result in failure.

Step 10: Evaluating the decision
Again assuming quantitative objectives, clear decisions and predefined control systems, evaluation is simple. The problems of control and evaluation are caused by lack of clear yardsticks against which to compare. If you simply set broad qualitative goals of increasing sales "as much as possible" or improving customer service, you will have the utmost difficulty in evaluating the results. There will usually be no common definition of what constitutes an increase or an improvement.

DEVELOP A CREATIVE APPROACH

Words like "creativity" and "innovation" invoke what sound like highly desirable attributes of both organisations and people. They also conjure up typecast images of the creative department in an advertising agency or the innovation inherent as a high-tech company exploits latest developments. Ideas come in all shapes and sizes (there is more about sources of ideas under the heading "Being Effective"); they can be revolutionary or may be better characterised as evolutionary, the gradual process of change and development by which so much that drives an organisation is carried forward. Most jobs involve some of this process, certain specialist areas consist mostly of this and, generally speaking, senior people tend to have need of the highest skills in this area.

It may be sensible in dealing with such broad concepts to define our terms: creativity is the thinking process that helps us generate ideas, whereas innovation is the practical application of such ideas towards meeting an organisation's objectives in an effective way. Innovation is thus the essence of corporate success, taking ideas and converting them into practical and workable ways forward. This being the case, individuals who have innovative and creative ways of approaching things tend to be favoured in choices affecting who rises through the ranks of an organisation. Clearly it follows that if you can develop this side of your abilities this may be something else favourable to your career.

Some faced with these comments abdicate all thoughts of success: "I am just not a creative person," they say, as if it were something you are born with like brown eyes or perfect pitch. Maybe; but there is another view which says you can work at it. Consider an analogy. When someone writes, say, a novel, something that in a different context would be regarded as a creative act, they need ideas. But they need other things as well, a process is involved which is to some degree structured. A story needs a beginning, a middle and an end. If it is dramatic each part will end with a cliffhanger or reversal, with the next section turning things round and taking the plot forward. There are a mass of principles about what makes a character, say, sympathetic and all this goes with the ideas that must be built in to create the whole. I know, I have had two novels published and "Long Overdue" is... sorry, I digress! Much innovation is not, in fact, creative in the sense of the wonderful new idea just popping ready made into someone's head. It is hard graft; it is the systematic working at something in the right way that produces results.

Perhaps producing results is the key. You may never be sufficiently creative to write a sonata that will still be well-thought-of in a hundred years' time, but you may well have to produce results for your organisation which cannot be done without some original thinking. This you can work at; after all it is not so much creativity which is the key - it is *creating*.

TAKE A BROAD VIEW

One of the things that differentiates management from direction (though not every director from every manager) is their ability to see – and take – the broad view. Again some will claim this is an inherent skill, others that it is something that can be developed. By broad I mean both in canvass and in time. An ability to do this is a characteristic shared by many entrepreneurs, or certainly the more successful of them. An initial idea or premise gives rise to a vision of where that can take them, the kind of organisation that can be built on it, the way it will work to create success and what it will bring in terms of rewards.

Someone has to handle the details as well, of course, but most jobs benefit from taking the broad view and anyone who can stand back, particularly from immediate concerns or problems, and get things in perspective is likely to increase their effectiveness. Sometimes achieving this only means curbing the natural tendency to "jump in". This can show itself in both positive and negative situations, if someone says, "What can we do to solve this?" the temptation is to focus hard up front on the problem and possible solutions, but such may come more readily if the problem is seen in context: why is this occurring? What are we trying to achieve? Similarly with opportunities: ask "What can we make of this?" The best response may be to consider hard whether making anything of it will fit in with the overall activity, rather than instantly suggesting three or four development possibilities. The same principle of thinking should span activities. General management must always think about finance, resources, people and the market and a dozen external factors and more, always with the precise combination of factors matching the subject of consideration. Most jobs demand their own particular span.

You may have such skills already or have them in embryo from; if so do cultivate them, consciously take a broad view even of matters within a smaller scale in your own part of an organisation; if not start to develop them, particularly if you have a directing role in mind for yourself.

So far so good, but while skills are necessary they need to be acquired, maintained and extended and it to this we turn next.

CHAPTER 6
TRAINING AND DEVELOPMENT

ACQUIRING, MAINTAINING AND EXTENDING SKILLS

Those in business are more and more well-qualified. A degree, or more specifically a business degree, is regarded as the basic by many organisations. But having such a qualification is no longer sufficient – education in business should have a practical bias. It was once said, probably by someone less well-qualified, that the perfect business enterprise was to set up a trading house that purchased MBAs for what they were worth and sold them for what they thought they were worth! The point being that the arrogance of the MBAs would ensure a significant profit. By and large those with such qualifications are also practical these days (though the fact of some such qualifications is no guarantee of this), but whatever your prime qualification it should be a beginning and not an end. Next we look at a number of career building factors to do with development.

Before we get into this however, it fits here to address the topic of job appraisals, which have a direct link to training and development.

USING APPRAISALS

This is not the place for me to commend to organisations the merits of a good appraisal system, one that makes a constructive contribution to maintaining and improving performance standards, though it may be worth noting that in my experience you are likely to encounter different kinds of appraisal in a career that spans a number of different employers. Not all of them will be effective, some managers are bad at conducting such meetings, and you may not feel all are constructive. So be it, careers do not progress in a perfect world, but you should seek to get the most from them whatever they are like. They should help you forward. Consider:

i) Appraisals: preparing for them

Be sure you understand how the appraisal system in your organisation works before you find yourself in the first such meeting. Incidentally, this is a good topic to investigate when you are being interviewed for a job, but before your first meeting you are likely to need more detailed information than is spelt out at that stage. Ask for information if this is not provided and ask some of your longer serving peers how their meetings go, how long they last and what they get from them. Particularly be sure you know *why* appraisals are done, *how* management conducting them views them, *what* they look to get from them, and *what* time span the review covers.

Then you can consider *how* you want the meeting to go and how you can influence it. For instance ask yourself what:

- You want to raise and discuss
- They are likely to raise (and responses to any negative areas that may come up)
- The link is between appraisal and, development and training, and what you hope to get in this area
- The link is between the meeting and your future work, responsibilities and projects undertaken
- Questions you want to ask.

And, if it is not your first appraisal, check what was said at and documented after the last one.

This must be done in the context of what you now know about the forthcoming appraisal. A couple of points are worth careful planning. One is the link to salary review and other benefits. Many organisations separate discussion of this from appraisal meetings (indeed there is a strong case for doing so), if this is the case it cannot be raised, except perhaps in general terms. If it will be discussed you may have things to prepare here also. Another key point is the make-up of the discussion in terms of time scale. A good appraisal will always spend more time on the future than on the past, both aspects need thought and certainly there is no excuse for your not having the facts at your fingertips about anything that is a likely candidate for discussion in the review of past events.

Make notes as you plan and take them with you - there is no point in trusting to memory and, in any case, being seen to have thought seriously about the meeting will benefit you. You may only get one, sometimes two, such opportunities in any one year. Therefore, some careful preparation will prevent the occasion being wasted.

ii) Appraisals: attending them

The person who is conducting the appraisal will have a bearing on both how it is done and how you need to conduct yourself. If it is with a manager with whom you are on good terms and see every day, this will make for a less formal meeting than if it is someone more senior with whom you only have occasional contact (numbers of appraisals involve three people including the person to be appraised). A good appraisal will:

- Be notified well in advance
- Have clear agenda
- Have a duration in mind.

And these are things you should ask for if necessary. Particularly you may want to have ideas about how much time will be spent discussing last year and next, how interactive the meeting is and when you can ask questions, perhaps also what is, and is not, on the record. Some appraisals are rather checklist in style: that is the appraiser leads and raises the points one at a time asking for your view or comment. Others are more open and allow the person being appraised to lead, pulling them back to an agenda only if the meeting digresses too much. Ideally you will know which way it runs, but you must be ready for either. Remember lack of comment may be read as lack of awareness, knowledge or as indecisiveness. On the other hand, if the question posed needs some thought then it is better to let the appraiser know rather than answering with a hasty comment.

Appraisals should not be traumatic occasions. If they are constructive – and prompting change in the future is the only real reason for doing them – then you can take a reasonably relaxed view of them (provided you have done some preparation) and there is no reason why you should not enjoy as well as find them useful. You are on show, career planning decisions are being made, albeit long term, by those conducting these meetings, but it is also a positive opportunity for you to present something of your competence in a way that goes "on the record".

iii) Appraisals: the follow up

Appraisals are too important to just file away in your mind or forget about once they are past. They can provide a catalyst to an ongoing dialogue during the year. In many organisations, the system demands that the appraiser documents proceedings, and usually that the appraisee confirms that this documentation is a true record of the salient issues.

But there is no reason why you cannot take the initiative on particular matters. Consider the following as an example. Development requirements are one topic that most appraisals review. This may result in specific action – "I will enroll you on that communication course next month" – or it may result

74

in further discussion, more than can be accommodated in the appraisal meeting itself. It may be useful to volunteer to undertake the processes involved (remember your boss could have a dozen appraisals in the same week and much attendant administration). If you put in a paper setting out some suggestions for action, and if this is used as the agenda for another session about it, then this could well see more of what you plan to happen happening, and happening sooner, than would otherwise be the case. Similarly use the opportunity to report back after any agreed training, in writing or at a meeting, so the dialogue continues. If the training has been agreed as successful then there is logic in discussing "what's next".

A final point – you may think attending them is a chore, but appraisals are not easy to conduct, take time to prepare and always seem to be scheduled during busy periods. So, if it has been useful, express thanks and if it has not, try to comment in a way that may set the scene for a more productive encounter next year.

ACCEPT AND LEARN FROM CRITICISM

A good appraisal is likely to be a good meeting. Even if it is poorly conducted and not really very constructive, it is a satisfying feeling to come out saying to yourself, "I did well", particularly when someone else has told you so. But unless you believe the graffiti which says "I used to be great but now I am absolutely perfect", few of us get through many such meeting without having to take some criticism. We must consider the possibility that it is fair comment. You are probably not perfect, you do not get everything right, excel in all you do and you sometimes get things wrong.

Because, perhaps understandably, no one likes having their failures, even minor ones, aired in public. There is a danger that you simply put such comment out of your mind and concentrate on the good things that are said (almost all appraisals will touch on both). Careers are not enhanced either by repeating mistakes or ignoring failings or weaknesses. If you do not take action after an appraisal and do so promptly, at least in terms of planning such action, then the moment will pass. Resolve to take note and, if necessary, action and you will do yourself and your career a favour.

ASSESS YOUR DEVELOPMENT NEEDS

To say you are actively developing your career in terms of training and everything that word implies, does not mean grabbing at every opportunity to, say, attend a course regardless of any consideration except that it is possible. You need to consider what development is necessary (which in job terms is what will happen at many organisation appraisal schemes). It is worth thinking this through in a systematic way and, of course, doing so honestly. Otherwise, your career will certainly suffer if you deceive yourself and ignore gaps in your knowledge or skills that are in fact necessary.

First, you should remember that development can only do three things:

- Improve your knowledge
- Develop your skills
- Change your attitudes

With that in mind, consider the thinking involved in defining training needs. This involves a ten-step process:

1. *Identify the requirements of your current job in terms of knowledge, skills and attitudes* – you need to be honest about this and think broadly about it (and it is definitely easier if you have a clear job description).
2. *Identify your own current level of such knowledge, skills and attitudes* – look at how well you can perform in your job now.

76

3. *Identify any additional factors indicated as necessary in future because of likely or planned changes* – in today's dynamic business climate there are likely to be some of these.
4. *Consider and add any additional aspects that your own longer term career plan demands* – this can look as far ahead as you wish, but realistically should concentrate on the shorter term.
5. *Set priorities* – note what needs to be done, there may well be more than it is realistic to change very quickly and you then need to set clear priorities to help you make progress.
6. *Set clear objectives* – always be absolutely clear what you are trying to do and why.
7. *Consider the timing* – in other words, when any development can take place, and this no doubt in a busy life means one thing at a time and perhaps at a slower pace than you would ideally like.
8. *Implement* – do whatever is necessary to complete the development involved. This could be very simple: you doing something that you can control. Or it could involve discussion and debate with others (e.g. your line manager) to get agreement about the need and to the necessary time and money.
9. *Evaluate* – this is an important one. Many people forget to really think through how useful and relevant something, like attending a course has been, when a little review can ensure much better linking to the real job and future tasks.
10. *Assess against the job/career factors* – as well as evaluating general usefulness of anything done, you need to match its effect with both current tasks and future career plans to see how well it helps with your specific work and plans.

Then you are back to the beginning again. The process is a continuous cycle: it is something where regular review is necessary, if not month by month then certainly year by year. Next you need to relate this to a plan and then think about the actions that are implied to see it through. We turn to these next.

HAVE A SELF-DEVELOPMENT PLAN

In today's dynamic world, development must be a continuous process. There will be new skills you need to acquire during your career and perennial skills to be kept up to date. If you are with an organisation that has a sound development policy, the thinking needed here may well be prompted by what action is forthcoming from such activity. If not, or is what is done is, in your view and for your needs, inadequate, then you will need to initiate what happens here. You need a plan. Not something cast in tablets of stone that stretches into the future and is unchangeable, but a rolling plan, something that sets out immediate actions or intentions clearly and an outline for the longer term. The detail of this will have to change as events unfold, and you must adjust to changing circumstances and needs. Some such changes are fairly long term.

Other changes may be more rapid, and still affect your development intentions. A move to an overseas office, perhaps, or the organisation setting up an overseas subsidiary might prompt thoughts about language skills. The options in terms of action are several:

* The organisation may suggest something (e.g. attendance on a course)
* You may want to suggest something to them
* You, or they, may want to amend or adapt an original suggestion

* You may conclude that whatever the company does, you will meet your own personal objectives, even working in your own time.

The permutations are, of course, many. The key thing is that you devote a little time regularly to considering what you feel would help. This means looking at immediate job advantages as well as long term career ones (after all your employer will be more inclined to spend money on things that have a reasonably short term impact for them, while you may want to look further ahead), and keeping your personal plan – which should be in writing – up to date.

There is an important link here with any job appraisal scheme which you find yourself taking part in – many organisations have their own schemes. Some consist of just an informal annual meeting, others are more formal and more regular. Such schemes, if they are good, are very much to be commended (and are dealt with separately). Whatever kind of scheme there is, it is likely that you will find it consists, in part, of a review of development needs. This is the moment to link your personal plan with that of the organisation for which you work. With the support and approval of your immediate boss, you will probably find you can do more that will benefit your current job and the tasks it entails and get more benefit for what will help you in the longer term.

Just as you need a career plan, you need a development plan. All business literature commends, indeed advocates, planning. This is not just because it is a formality that the academic texts insist on; it really works. If you take a moment to keep your thoughts straight about this area, you will be better able to action more of what you want and better able also to take advantage of circumstances.

A final point: some development is interesting, some may even be fun. That is all well and good, but it does not mean it all will be. Some of the most useful developmental activities can be a chore; so be it, if it must be done, it must be done. You may not know what skills or knowledge will change your own work pattern in future – but beware of putting off acquiring new skills because the process of doing so is a chore.

READ A BUSINESS BOOK; REGULARLY

As I make my living, in part, by writing this may seem like a plug, but this is certainly amongst the simplest forms of development and a good deal can be learnt from it. It takes some time but is also something that you can allocate to certain moments when perhaps time would otherwise be wasted. Such time includes traveling, and I know more than one salesperson who always carries a business book to read in those, sometimes long, moments he regularly spends in his customers' reception areas.

The first rule is to make it a habit. Always have such a book on the go (even if it takes you a while to get to the end) and keep watching for what is current in book shops, by reading the reviews in the press and getting yourself added to publishers' mailing lists, Amazon is a useful source.

There are two kinds of book to concentrate on. The first consists of those titles that link directly to your development need, like *Smart skills: Persuasion* (also in this series). These may be immediate needs or something you wish to develop further ahead. Remember it may be useful to come at things in different ways, the constructive repetition involved will help you take in the message, so it is worth reading more than one title on certain topics.

The second category are those books that are better described as background reading; so if you want to know about the publishing industry try *The Merchants of Culture* (John B. Thompson, Polity Press). This may seem a small point but applied conscientiously its effect may be considerable. A book every quarter, for instance, is still quite an input of information over say five years of your career. Six a year is better still.

ATTEND A COURSE

Courses, seminars, workshops – whatever word you use attendance on these events can be very beneficial. And in the long run a couple of days spent on such an event is not too high a price to pay compared to what may be gained from them. Some employers will regularly give you the opportunity to attend both external courses or those set up and run only for their personnel; if not you may want to prompt them. If you are making such suggestions, particularly to attend outside events, remember you must put your case persuasively. Just ask to attend and some of the thoughts that come to mind may be negative: "He wants my job", "Once she has extended her skills a little more she will be likely to leave the organisation". Tell them what *they* will get. Explain what more you will be able to do for them and for the organisation; will you be more effective, more productive, able to save or make money?

Choose carefully. If you make wild suggestions, something that clearly only benefits you in the long term or ask to attend something every week, you are unlikely to get agreement. Make practical suggestions and get approval and you perhaps create the right kind of precedent and habit. I remember once battling for three years for the budget and time to attend a conference in the United States. Once I had been and it proved useful, then it rapidly moved to being a regular event. Certainly the most important consideration is the topic and the content, but realistically there are other things to think about: who is organising it, speaking at it and attending it? The style of events is important also; I am not alone for example in finding some to the best known "gurus" disappointing in the flesh. You may want something with an international flavour or with specific relevance to your own industry or activity.

One single new idea, or even one single existing idea confirmed with sufficient weight to prompt you into action in some particular area, is all that is necessary to make this process worthwhile and at best there is a great deal to be gained by it. The next three sections investigate specific aspects of course attendance.

CONDUCT YOURSELF RIGHT AT COURSES

It is said that you only get out of something what you put in. Certainly this is true of course attendance. First, once attendance is fixed, you should think through what you want to get from it. This will help you and the course tutor – I know my heart sinks if I ask people on seminars which I conduct why they are present and their only answer amounts to "I was told to be here". Never go to a seminar without a written note of your objectives and any specific questions you want to obtain comments on. Most lecturers are happy to get a note of questions in advance, but in my experience this is rarely done.

Thereafter you need to think about how you will behave "on the day". If the programme is internal, you may know all the other participants and the whole tenor of the event may be informal. If it is external, it can be a little daunting to arrive in a room of participants none of whom you know. Everyone is in the same situation, however, and the informal contacts and the comments and shared experience of your fellow participants may be an important part of your attendance. This makes, I think, a useful point about being open-minded and adopting an approach which is constructive. In view of the time and cost of attending such events, it is a great pity to walk away at the end with some key question still unanswered.

It is important to adopt the right approach. Time on such an event goes all too quickly and it is easy to leave and then wish you had asked something else. Try not to worry about what people will think. Sometimes you may feel others are all ahead of you in understanding. Often they are not and the question postponed, because it seemed obvious and likely to make you appear stupid, actually once asked, proves to be a common question which leads into very useful discussion for all.

MAXIMISE COURSE ATTENDANCE BENEFITS

The most important thing about any course you may attend is what happens after it is finished. Courses may be interesting, they may even be fun, but what really matters at the end of the day is the action they prompt. So even more important than the notes you make before attending is the action plan you make afterwards.

Compiling such a plan has to start at once. It is inevitably for most that if you are away for even a couple of days at a short course you are going to have more in the in-tray on your desk afterwards than if you had not attended. Yet the moment to start any action resulting from the course is the following day. Nothing later will do, the likelihood is that you will get involved in catching up and everything will be put on one side and forgotten.

So whatever else you do, take ten minutes on the day after attendance to list – in writing – the areas of action you noted during the programme. At least get them on your "to do" list whether they are things to think about, to review further or to take action on; whether they represent things you can implement solo or things you will need support or permission for and must raise at the next appropriate meeting. If you do this much and then approach them systematically and with an eye on the priorities something is more likely to happen. If you miss this stage, the danger is not that you will do less, but that you will do nothing.

So, follow up your notes, do not just make good intentions but firm action plans and consider also:

• Reviewing and keeping safe any course notes that were useful

- Having a de-briefing session with your boss, the training manager or whoever sent you. If they are convinced it was useful, then future requests may be that much easier to make and get agreed. When this is done is worth considering. There cannot be much implemented action to report immediately after attendance, but your recall of the detail will be greater. Later on, you can review what you have done as a result more realistically. Thus two meetings may be worthwhile. If your company asks you to complete an appraisal form about the course attended, always do so thoroughly and on time; they are useful in a large organisation to the process of deciding what training is used in the future. Not doing this may be seen as indicating you have no interest in training.

Also, from a career record point of view, file away details of the course (and maybe the certificate of attendance) and add it to a list you can keep with your C.V. This is worthwhile as the memory fades quickly. Five years on when someone asks what you know about X, it may be useful to look up exactly when you attended a course on the topic and what it covered.

Just attending a developmental event is nearly always useful; if it is a well-chosen and practical one it may be very useful; and if you go into the process with the right attitude and take the right action before, during and after the event, you will maximise the benefit that comes from it.

GO ON LEARNING – AT A DISTANCE

Change, including technological change, affects almost everything in our lives, including education and training. One format established in this area is what is called "distance learning". This is a rather imprecise term that covers a range of rather different things, but the principle in all cases is similar - that of receiving some kind of formal training (including education resulting in a qualification) by working alone linked to, but not actually attending, the establishment providing the tuition.

The options are many and varied and allow you to study part time while continuing to work full time and develop your career on the job front. You can undertake anything from an MBA to a short course covering some individual skill area. The form of the course will include conventional study, with things to read, but may also involve a series of other methodologies: videos, exercises, programmed learning and, in the best formats, the ability to complete projects and papers that are sent away and then receive individual critique and comment to help you through the whole exercise. Some courses also involve some group activity, weekend sessions are sometimes used to fit this aspect in without making it impossible for those working full time to attend.

The area is worthy of some investigation for anyone wishing to extend their learning. But, a word of caution – because of the profusion of material that has become available, there is, amongst excellent material and schemes, some that is frankly not so good. A good deal of work is involved in any lengthy distance learning course so it is worth selecting what you do carefully, and there are also considerable differences in costs.

Like anything you may do to bolster your learning there is a perception involved. The course may be good, you learn something that will benefit your career. In addition, the fact of your doing it, and the commitment clearly implied, makes a point to people and this too may count on your overall record. There are some institutions and providers that are more likely to make this kind of impact than others. So the total basis of choice must allow all these factors.

TAKE ON NEW THINGS

Make a point of taking on new things. Experience and the range of your competence are both things that must be kept moving, like sharks which must keep swimming or sink. There is a temptation in many jobs to stick with the areas of work which are "safe", by which I mean where you do not have to stretch and where you are sure of what you can do. This is almost always a mistake. Allowing that if you spread your learning too wide you may end up with some expertise across too broad a front rather than a real strength in particular areas, an on-going objective to broaden your range of skills, expertise and experience is likely to be helpful to you in the long run. As the US novelist Henry James said, "*Experience is never limited, and it is never complete*"; not only is the potential for broadening yourself vast, so are the possibilities of something added to your range of abilities acting to make a positive career change.

You never know what the future holds and, at the risk of sounding very old, it is an easy mistake amongst the young to rule out possibilities on the grounds of some inherent prescience. I know from my own experience that skills that have helped me more recently in my career formed no part of my expertise early on and, with hindsight, I do not think I predicted what would be useful in this sort of way. So, next time something new is on offer, something that will stretch your powers and even where the outcome is somewhat more certain, think very carefully before you decide to avoid it or say "no". You could be taking on something that will kick-start your career into its next move forward.

CHAPTER 7
BEING EFFECTIVE

FOCUS ON AND ACHIEVING RESULTS

There is a saying that one must never confuse activity with achievement. It is true. Never deceive yourself that being busy, applying yourself, putting in the hours or whatever, scores many points. It may not score any. What is noticed is results. When it is said, within a particular organisation, that promotion is "on merit", it means, putting it bluntly, that you will only make progress if you succeed in your current role. So things that improve your effectiveness will, in turn, help your career. That is dependent on your expertise in your chosen role. Here we review some common factors that will help everyone's progress.

RECOGNISE AND ACCEPT PARETO'S LAW

This principle, named after the famous Italian economist Vilfredo Pareto, is more popularly known as the 80/20 rule. It has various applications in business and here can be related to the fact that only 20 per cent of what you do will have a real effect on results. It is the root cause of the fact that some people in business always seem to complete those things that bring them recognition, and others never seem to be other than hidden behind a never reducing "pending" tray. This is true of both time and effort. This may sound harsh, after all you are no doubt busy most of the time and everything seems important in the moment, but the principle is a strong one. While the figures will not be exactly 80/20, something close to the ratio will be the case; the rule is true. What is more it can be applied to specific areas of work as well: for example 20 per cent of meeting time produces 80 per cent of the decisions (and very probably 20 per cent of the areas in this book will be more relevant and useful to you than the rest). Every job includes numbers of essential activities, those that are key to achieving what the job demands, as well as a profusion of minor activities which, though they have to be done, do not contribute in the same way to success.

Recognising this is itself a significant step to ensuring that the 20 per cent is given due consideration and that, in turn, should prompt you to have a very serious look at time management (discussed next), for both can have a direct effect on your effectiveness and therefore on your being seen to achieve objectives.

MANAGE YOUR TIME EFFECTIVELY

In business, you will have noticed that some people seem to manage their time better than others. Like so much else, this does not just happen. And it is without doubt one of *the* key factors governing success in work and in career. If two people have the same skills and, all other things being equal (which they are not, of course, but the point remains), one manages their time better than the other - then they may well also make better progress. Managing your time effectively not only allows you to be more productive, doing more as well as being able to concentrate on the key tasks (see the above section on Pareto's Law), it will most likely be noticed; it labels you as an achiever.

This is perhaps the classic area of good intentions. Everyone says they are going to manage their time well. Some buy expensive time management systems. But if I had the price of a beer for everyone who has said that and not, if they are honest, done anything about it, then I could have retired instead of writing this book! No system will do it for you – time management is about self-management and therefore about self-discipline. This means it is a habit and, as such, while it may take effort to acquire, the whole process does become easier once you have made a commitment and done some ground work. What are the key disciplines?

First, you must plan to plan. You need a system, and it can be a loose leaf diary or notebook rather than a generic system, that allows you to note what you have on the go, to prioritise it and to progress it. Sensibly it will link to a diary. I have yet to meet anyone who can truly hold all this in their memory, though some claim to do so, otherwise some record is therefore always necessary in writing. The second rule is to update your plan regularly. How long this takes will depend on the job you do. For the majority of people no more than five minutes will be necessary each day. When you do this is a matter of personal preference – first thing in the morning or as you pack up for the day are favoured by many.

So far so good and now the next step. You simply have to do what the plan says! This, of course, is where it tends to become difficult. So many things conspire to stop you and it is here that the classic timewasters need controlling: too much time in unproductive meetings, too many interruptions, too much repetitive administration. You can – must – work at all of these, but two things especially need watching which you can control:

- Putting off what you dislike or find difficult – it is constantly thinking about a task, shuffling papers, but coming to no conclusion or action that wastes so much time.
- Spending too much time on the things you like, and this often means the things you believe no one else is able to do as well as you. This is often the worse of the two problems.

If you have ever attended a time management course, you will certainly have been encouraged to keep a time log. It is always a sobering exercise; try it for a couple of weeks and you will soon see where time goes. Almost always there are surprises; some things take up very much more time than you think. If you know how you work and what happens to your time, you can work at the details that will make you more productive.

In a sense, it really is true to say "that's all there is to it". Time management may be a struggle to get organised, but the principles are, for the most part common sense. Two final points: do not think that because much of your job is unplannable (perhaps because it is reactive, like the manager of a customer service department who must take customer calls and respond at once, but also has longer term tasks to plan out and fit in) that you cannot manage it. You must plan the non-reactive time, and the less you have of it the more important it is to utilise it effectively. And consider the old maxim that there is never time to do something properly but always has to be time to do something again. Regularly you will find that to sort something may take half an hour or an hour instead of ten minutes. The temptation is to get it done and out of the way, rather than pause and take longer. Take that time once, however, and you may save five minutes every day in future. That may not sound much, but given the average number of working days in the year you save around 20 hours; maybe every year thereafter.

This is a most important area. Unless you get to grips with it you will be at a serious disadvantage vis a vis those who do. Become a master of your time and you become able to be more effective; both your results and the way you are seen will improve and this is one more help to an advancing career.

USING INFORMATION

There is a saying for every occasion, and one such that is most certainly true in the context of corporate careers is:

information is power. At the risk of quoting too much, the other well-known saying that has relevance here was something said by Dr. Samuel Johnson: "We know a subject ourselves, or we know where we can find information upon it." In other words, what matters is not simply the information you have, but knowing where to find what you do not have. You need your wits about you to make progress in many organisations and without doubt, one way in which this manifests itself is in the information you can marshal together, and which you can do without hassle or delay. It is often said as a compliment that someone has "all the facts at his fingertips". Here we look at three factors that you need to consider:

i) Decide what you need to know

The first step, if you are to have "everything at your fingertips", is to decide what you need to know and particularly to decide what is most important and thus must be kept in mind or close at hand. Like it or not, in common with everyone else on the planet, your mind does not have an infinite memory and often it does not have an infallible one (more of this later). Nor do you have unlimited storage in your office, so you must decide what you are going to keep.

There can be no list here that is right for everyone and what you need will vary depending on your job, your employer and the stage of your career you are at. It may well vary as time goes by on both long and short-term scales. Some categories may help, however:

- Policy and guidelines – some of these you need in mind, the rest nearby; you will not endear yourself to the boss or anyone else if you are constantly checking the policy on routine matter, less so if you apply it incorrectly.
- Figures – statistics, sales or productivity figures, ratios, percentages; every business and every department has some that are important.
- Records – anything from a contract to a schedule.

- Personal details (we picked this up in the section on people).

The trick is not simply to decide the categories that are important to you, but to decide what and how much to keep on different topics and in different files. Only about ten per cent of everything put into a filing system is ever looked at again, and there is no real reason to feel that other organisations are radically different. So, seemingly you can throw away ninety per cent of all the information you hold on file. Actually the problem is not so simple; first you need to consider – *which* is the ten per cent you need to keep. There is a serious point here. Some people seem to keep much less than others yet always have to hand what is required; it is a habit and way of viewing things which can be developed and it is very useful too – one that you would do well to develop.

ii) Obtain the right information
The information base that you need will not just arrive on your desk as if by magic. A fair amount can go in that invaluable filing system WPB (the waste paper basket). Other information you will need to seek out. One-off things have to be dealt with as they arise, regular things are worth a comment. Get yourself on any:

- Internal circulation list
- Supplier mailing lists (catalogues, etc.)
- Magazine subscription or circulation lists that will produce useful information for you.

Consider anything and everything else that will help you keep up-to-date and well-informed: directories, yearbooks, association membership lists, information services, and keep a note of apparently one-off sources – both internally and externally – that could be useful again in the future.

Review all these regularly – it is yet something else that

must become a habit. Not only will having good information and knowing where to find out the other things you want help you directly, there is usually no harm in becoming known within an organisation as a source of information. Carefully used, this can keep you in touch with the right people but watch out it does not lead to time wasting.

iii) Do the necessary research

Sometimes the information which may support your cause will not exist in your system or indeed elsewhere internally. You should resolve to augment what you have with such research as is necessary to update or complete what you have. Never risk basing a case, perhaps for a project or change of responsibilities, on uncertain data. This means you need a line into probably a number of sources of information. What these may be will depend entirely on the area in which you work and the kind of information you are likely to need. In addition to the ubiquitous websites, such may include other companies, libraries, institutes or trade and industry bodies – and also helpful individuals. People are usually flattered to be regarded as an expert in their field; so, provided you are an appreciative contact (they are not adverse to the occasional thank you) this is certainly possible to build up.

If you can put yourself in the position where some of this is done on an exchange or favour basis so much the better. It is very useful to be able to lift the phone to a friend or acquaintance and borrow a report, check a figure or whatever may be necessary. A reputation for basing everything you do on hard facts is a good one to cultivate. The trick is to make such information easy, quick and inexpensive to come by; and ensure the accuracy and quality involved is good. If you achieve that, such a network can be a real asset.

Note: however you find information, if it's useful you need to be able to locate it easily and promptly. File things regularly, sensibly and systematically therefore and keep files up to date (which means cleaning stuff out as well as putting material in). This applies to both paper and, perhaps especially, electronically stored material. As a final thought consider how much information is on your computer and how easy or difficult it is to locate specific items.

NEVER FORGET COMMITMENTS

In my first job (as a lowly "management trainee") I became convinced my boss had an infallible memory or used something akin to magic. He *never* seemed to forget anything. He would ask me to do something: "Have a think about it and we will discuss it at the end of the month," he would say. And come the day if I was not at his office door with it at 9:00 a.m., the phone on my desk would ring and he would say, "Now, what about the discussion we planned..." He would do this with a couple of dozen people all around the office, registering many, many points with each and doing so in both directions. In other words, if he told you he would let you have something or would do something – whatever – he would do it; and on the rare occasions where something prevented it, he would forewarn you of it.

This is a good characteristic to find in a boss and it is a good one to display to a boss. Reliability is approved; it is efficient – knowing something will be as planned may be important – and it keeps the majority of contacts you have with more senior managers positive. You do not want their automatic recall of you to be of the endless chasers which they have to make but which they regard as unnecessary.

My boss owed none of his reputation in this area to magic. He simply had a good system. He had a page in a loose-leaf diary for each person who worked for him, and kept a record of projects large and small linked to his diary. It worked well, and if you build up the reputation of always honouring commitments, whichever way round, that will work well for you.

ALWAYS HIT DEADLINES

Although deadlines are commitments, timing is worth a word in its own right. You do not just need to remember and do *what* the commitment entails but do it by *when* it was arranged. It is said there was never a deadline in history that was not negotiable. This may be true and there is certainly no merit in being pushed somehow into agreeing to a deadline that you cannot possibly meet. It may need negotiation, or at least discussion. Once set, however, a deadline – your deadline – takes on another characteristic, it becomes irrevocable. It can do your reputation nothing but good to be known as someone who delivers on time – not just the major projects and not just when senior people are involved, but everything. Once you have said, "I will make sure you have it on Friday week" or something similar, everyone should *know* it will be there.

Always think through any task before agreeing to any particular timing. The more complex the task, the more important this is. Something may appear straightforward, but it is only when you reach stage four perhaps that complications set in and this needs to be built into your estimate of how long it will take – no doubt amongst the other things you have on your plate. Sometimes in organisations, there is a confusing incidence of what might be called "deadline abuse". That is, someone wants something on, let us say, 31 May, so they build in a safety factor and say they need it by 25 May. But people know this is what happens, so it is accepted with the thought that he always builds in a week or so, and that the 2/3 June will do. If more people are involved then this scenario rapidly gets much more complicated and the only thing you can be sure of is that there will be a muddle. Deadlines should be honestly stated and then dealt with accordingly.

Treat deadlines with care and you will help your colleagues and others on who are dependent on them being hit, and that in turn will help you.

DECIDE THE RIGHT PRIORITIES

First things first it is said. Which is a reminder of another area which may be viewed as part of time management, the simple matter of setting priorities. Simple may seem the wrong choice of word and, of course, priority setting is not necessarily easy. But it is simple fact of life that you can only complete one task at a time. First you do one thing and then you do another, and another. Sometimes you have to pause to tackle something else – this may be an interruption like a telephone call, but, for the moment it becomes a priority (otherwise you should offer to call back later!). A great deal of time is often spent by busy people in trying to achieve impossibilities. If you can only do one thing at a time (and you can) then you must decide which task takes priority. Of course you may be progressing a number of things at the same time and this must be built into the decision.

Some things need more time spent on them than others. It may be a priority to make a promised telephone call to someone on a particular day. It will take only a few minutes. Another task, like writing this book, may well have a deadline but the work needs to be spread over a large number of days. When things change, and you accept and add a new priority, you need to recalculate. For example, if I promise to deliver the manuscript for this book on a set date and things I could not predict at the time interfere, then there are not so many options. I can work harder, long into the evening perhaps; I can delay some other task or I can delay the deadline. The temptation is to struggle on trying to do far too much for a while and then end up with something, or several some-thing's, done inadequately.

Those with whom you work would no doubt love it if nothing unpredictable happened in your life and you were able to do everything exactly as you wanted. For the most part they do understand that this is simply not real life; changes do occur. Realistically, to return to my example it may be better for me to say to the publisher a month ahead of the deadline, "I am afraid I will be a week late", than to struggle on attempting to meet the time and end up not only missing it, but giving them no notice and perhaps making a mess of some other task along the way.

There is much talk these days of management stress and of managing it, books are written about it and courses conducted on it. But stress is, it seems to me, a reaction to circumstances rather than what the circumstances actually do to you. Clear job definition and clear objectives, mentioned earlier, should make it easier to decide priorities. Certainly a realistic attitude to how you arrange your work and what gets done first, second and third makes for greater effectiveness. Nothing is achieved just by panicking or sitting around and wondering what to do or wishing the priority decision did not have to be made. Concern and constructive thought about how to sort something are positive, worry is negative. What do all these have to do with your career?

Rapid and clear decisions made about your priorities – a continual process for most busy executives (often noted in time management systems) – will make you more effective. Clarity of thought, and decisiveness are both qualities looked for in more senior management. Learning to be philosophic about the things that cause stress, and concentrate your thinking on the practicalities of what will work best will reduce worry and get more done. And the whole thrust of this section is to show how increased effectiveness and the impression that it gives improves your career prospects.

HITTING TARGETS

In many organisations the culture is, in one respect, very straightforward. People who hit targets are regarded as achieving something and doing what is required. This is most obvious where there are numbers involved. If productivity was targeted to go up ten per cent but goes up eleven per cent instead, then this is good. And it is always clearest of all when the target is financial. It is, after all, money which keeps the wheels of most organisations turning. So someone on the sales side consistently hitting their sales target is much more likely to be promoted than a colleague whose results are down, and consistently missing target in such an area is often the best route to early "retirement". This is a powerful career influencer, and if you doubt just how powerful then, again, on the sales side you can note that it is quite often seen that the best salesman in an organisation is promoted but may then make a poor sales manager (after all the qualities and tasks the two jobs require are very different).

The career implications of this are very clear. Because you are significantly more likely to register as doing a good job if you are consistently hitting your target (much more so than in a, perhaps apparently appealing laissez-faire situation) you may want to consider:

- Suggesting that your job should include some targets if it does not – especially, if possible, financial ones – or indeed putting some numbers to it and suggesting the actual targets.
- Making sure any such targets are realistic, especially targets that someone else does set upon you. Some review, indeed some negotiation, here may be advisable.
- Making sure any such agreed targets are regularly reviewed, and also reported, although crowing about them too loudly if they are hit may be self-defeating.

Some would even say that jobs where measurement of success is inherently difficult are to be avoided, though such a job may offer other advantages. Generally speaking though a target hit or exceeded is always useful to the careerist; it is also motivational, most of us like to know all is going well rather than just to believe it is.

DO MORE THAN IS EXPECTED OF YOU

This seems an obviously good thing, and certainly there are derogatory remarks that conjure up the opposite, we talk for instance of people "scraping through", just doing sufficient to get by. This latter is not the attitude upon which careers thrive. So, delivering more than others expect is, not surprisingly, to be recommended.

This does not mean, however, that work has to take over your life and that "more" is produced as a result of excessive hours worked. It seems to be a fact that all the jobs which themselves are interesting or worthwhile do demand more than the regular "9 to 5" attitude (certainly this is my experience; if you have found something that is interesting, pays well and makes few demands please let me know!). So, accepting that, you need to be sufficiently industrious to create the right results and the right image. Remember there are two sides to every coin. Being consistently in the office for over long hours could be taken as a sign of inefficiency and that you are unable to cope.

Probably the most important way to deliver more is to think more about things than is necessary to do the job. For example, imagine you are asked to write a report on how your department's efficiency might be improved. This could be entirely introspective and based in the present, and you can come up with some perfectly good ideas for reducing costs or whenever the brief might be. Or it could take a broader view; maybe improvements are only possible by two departments working more closely together, or maybe there are advantages to be taken that link in and are made possible by events you know are coming in future. I am not suggesting the specifics of this example apply everywhere, but the process of thinking involved is clear and such may well produce more.

The same principle applies to seemingly much smaller issues. I sit on a small committee, and the chairperson of it always produces and circulates in advance a detailed agenda. It is not strictly necessary in terms of the complexity of the issues, but it is useful to those present – the chairperson does just a little more than is strictly necessary, and it shows. Be known as one who operates this way and it will be one more thing that can help you to be seen in the right light.

BE OPEN-MINDED

Nothing will stultify effectiveness and progress inside an organisation more than a closed mind. There is a saying that you can either have, say, five years' experience, or the same years' experience repeated five times. A closed mind goes through the same processes and thus the same experience. It is a cliché to say that we live in dynamic times and that the pace of change is increasing, but that does not mean it is not true. The open-minded will cope better with changes. You will have to accept, get to grips with and use new approaches, ideas and technologies in the future. You may already see some of these looming and others may be difficult if not impossible to imagine or predict today, but they will come nevertheless.

You must constantly take on board new ideas if your career is to progress, sometimes these will be major areas, as above, at other times it is a question of minor, but significant points – finding a way to work with a new, and seemingly difficult colleague perhaps. Whatever the job you do there will be these changes to cope with. There is a saying that if you have not changed you mind about something or adopted a new view recently, you should check your pulse – you may be dead! You must not get set in your ways so that you do not respond positively to these developments large and small, and like so much else you must be seen to be open-minded. It will secure your effectiveness over both the short and long term and make a contribution to the way your career progresses.

BE HONEST

"Honesty is the best policy" and in business, this is usually the case. I suppose I must say usually, because it is sadly true to say there are some people in some organisations who rise up the ranks and do well on out and out deception. It happens. And many of us have probably come across people who fall into this category. Not only that, but there are areas where large numbers of people are regularly dishonest. On C.V.s for instance, people claim to have degrees from universities which they have never attended, and to speak foreign languages of which they know not a word. In U.K. research has shown more than 15% of C.V.s contain lies.

So the truth of the matter is that while you may prosper by lying, you only have to get found out once and any good it may have done in the past is lost forever. In any case most want to achieve whatever they do on their own merits, there can surely be no real and lasting satisfaction in conning your way through; besides in many circumstances you are either honest or you are fired.

Honesty is the best policy, not least people around you should know that you are honest and keep your word, honesty links to trust which is an important factor in getting on in any organisation.

CHAPTER 8
YOUR PERSONAL PROFILE

BEING *SEEN* TO BE GOOD

It is sometimes said, for example of advertising, that "perception is reality". In other words, people will usually base their judgement on what they see of something. So too with people. Think of someone in your organisation perhaps whom you do not know very much about. Ask yourself what you think about them: are they busy? Competent? Approachable? Expert? Ambitious? Efficient? What do you think their staff think of them? And more. You will find that if you make yourself draw conclusions from any evidence, a reasonable picture builds up. You feel that you can judge something about them. Whether it is true or not is, of course, another matter.

Our very visibility gives out many signals and will do so whether we think about it consciously or not. Here we review some of the ways in which you can give signals that paint the right kind of picture of you and how you work that will create an image compatible with your career intentions.

LOOK THE PART

First impressions are largely visual and they are important. So too is someone's prevailing style, how colleagues and others see you around the office and work environment. Now this is a difficult area to advise on precisely. I am not promoting designer fashion or any specific style of dress, and you have to be reasonably natural, but you want to be seen to take business seriously.

You can be smart without spending a fortune; you must always be clean and tidy and the details matter. The Americans, who have a jargon phrase for everything, talk about "power dressing". This is a concept that is too contrived for many; indeed there is a real likelihood that going too far in this way becomes self-defeating, and is just seen as pretentious. It may be important in some jobs to meet the standards and style of those with whom the organisation does business rather than internally; for example customers. Once having met with a major bank to discuss possible training work, a colleague of mine, one who took a pride in his appearance, was dismayed that a letter came back requesting the work to be done by someone "shorter in the hair and longer in the tooth"! An older and more traditional alternative was found and the work went well; that is the client's right.

So, what specifically is certain? The following are often mentioned: clean finger nails and neat hair, smart (rather than over fashionable) clothes and clean shoes. Also, though it is more difficult to judge, an appropriate spend (I once had an enquiry for someone who said: "One of your competitors has just been to see me and arrived in a Porsche: I think I would like another quote.").

Finally, styles and norms differ internationally – a suit was once normal business dress in England, jacket and trousers (not a matching suit) is seen as just as acceptable as a suit in Holland, shirts and ties are more important in countries where the hot weather precludes jackets – and they differ in different kinds of business – generally a bank, say, being more formal than an advertising agency. Similarly men and women have different styles to consider, with the greater choice facing the women frankly making their choices more difficult. In recent years the trend has been towards less formality, though it may be safest not to opt for the least formality that seems to be acceptable.

Whatever your style, whatever you opt for, think about it and remember your appearance says very much more about you than you might think. You will have an image; the only question is what image you will make it.

CREATE EXTERNAL VISIBILITY

I once did a radio interview at which I remember meeting another interviewee who was there to comment on some technical matter. We got chatting and I asked him who he was. He said that he worked for a large company and had made a point of becoming known as the company's expert on the particular technical issue in question. "Do you run the technical department?" I asked him. "No", he said. "But I will one day." Investigating what he did to establish himself as the technical "guru", I was inclined to believe him.

He made a good point – public relations is not only a valuable tool to promote the company, it has career development potential as well. It is tightly linked with some of the communications skills reviewed earlier. My fellow interviewee at the radio studio would not have been there unless he could talk fluently about his chosen topic, just being knowledgeable about it was not enough. What is more, if he performed well then he stood a good chance of being asked back.

Radio is perhaps a dramatic example to take, though by no means unattainable, but public relations activity incorporates many different possibilities. Given that you have or can create some expertise worthy of comment, and very many jobs have this possibility, start internally as you review the possibilities. Is there a company magazine or newsletter? Are there groups or committees you can take part in or speak at? Then externally, should you be seeking to write articles, lecture at the local management institute or trade or professional body? This is very much an activity that creates its own momentum. For example, an article published in the company newsletter might be adapted to go in an external publication, a copy of that sent to a professional body might prompt an invitation to speak and at that meeting you might meet some who... but you get the point.

If such activity grows up naturally and has a use for the organisation as well as for you, then it should not create ripples (though someone may well wish they had thought of it first) and it can become an ongoing part of what you do to say to those about you that you are going places. Nothing succeeds like success they say and being seen to have achieved these things is certainly potentially useful. See you in the studio.

TAKE AN INTEREST IN YOUR INTERESTS

In some companies, particularly large ones, there is considerable social interaction amongst staff. Just how much are there and how it works will vary and is affected by such things as whether there is a social club and where the office is located: some city centre locations where people typically travel long distances to work may mean they live as much as a hundred miles apart and this will reduce social possibilities. There will also be a culture within the organisation relating to this kind of activity. In some companies, senior people are involved in some of this and others are clearly expected to be. In others, it is seen as a lower level activity and you may not want to get too involved in case you are seen as essentially frivolous.

Another issue here is that, rightly or wrongly, executives have a total image. Though interference in employees' private lives is not the style of most organisation, and would be resented by many staff, you may be expected to have certain interests. Some of these are perfectly reasonable; it is useful for executives, especially those who have contact outside the firm, to be generally well-informed in terms of current affairs, for example. If you are in a technical area, you may need to keep up-to-date on a broad range of scientific matters simply to be able to relate well to others you work with. On the other hand, there are organisations where the style of the chief executive – evidenced by a passion for, say, golf, science fiction or undersea diving – is mirrored by aspiring staff around the office forever plunging into the sea or Arthur C Clarke.

Whether this last is useful or not is uncertain. I would like to think it is not, but there are organisations where this kind of fitting in is important. It is certainly worth a thought. You are unlikely to have to rearrange your whole life around such things, but some accommodation with such perception may be useful.

DO NOT DRINK IN EXCESS

This is common sense, but worth a word. In many workplaces a certain amount of socialising is not only pleasant, it is part of the way the business works. On the other hand few, if any, decisions are helped by being the worse for drink and most, if not everyone in management will prefer to promote the office cat before promoting someone with even a hint of a drink problem. Enough said.

GIVE RATHER THAN TAKE

It would be difficult and, given the many different types of job and styles of organisation in the world, not even helpful to set out a perfect package of characteristics for those wanting to develop their careers. On point is, however, worth a thought. It may seem that a dedication to developing a career demands a selfish outlook, and to some degree this may be true. But think also of the effect a selfish attitude in others has on you. It is not the most endearing characteristic imaginable.

Success and effectiveness is assisted by cooperation,

teamwork has been mentioned elsewhere, and a selfish attitude to others hardly makes their cooperation in ways that will help you or your organisational objectives a forgone conclusion.

When I first went into consulting, I worked with a group of people who were less selfish than any other I have encountered before or since. No one ever seemed too busy to help. You could walk into any office and get advice, information and support of all kinds - from just a word to a complete run down on something. Information was regarded as for sharing not for exclusive hording and the whole firm, far from grinding to a halt because time was taken in this way, seemed to thrive on the attitude. For a newcomer, it was a godsend and I made full use of the learning and accelerated experience it provided and, in due course, found myself part of the network spending time giving as well as receiving.

There is an altruistic side to this attitude. You never know in an organisation how things will go and how things will turn out. The person whose head you bite off because they want a moment of your time when you are busy, turns up next a year later in a position of authority or influence and with not the slightest intention of sharing anything with you. You cannot have too many allies and you need to assess and deal with any opposition. The reverse applies also and this is one way that, whilst benefiting the company, cultivates more allies than enemies.

AVOID BEING TYPECAST

Every kind of business activity seems to run this risk. In my own business, it is very difficult to stop some clients seeing me exclusively as a consultant, others seeing me exclusively as a trainer or writer (though I work at it!). Some companies have a similar problem in selling the range of what they make, they are known for one, or two, main items and the others always seem to get left behind. There can be a similar situation with people as a career progresses, and sometimes the effect can be negative.

For example, the Greeks (or was it the Romans?) used to execute messengers bringing bad news. It cannot have made the bad news go away but it must, I suppose, have made them all feel better; well, all except the messengers! In a company people can take on a series of tasks, tasks which play to their strengths, are important and have to be done, but which tend to create a negative image of the individual. If you become known as the person who closed down the troublesome plant, made 300 people redundant, axed the firm's oldest and dearest product, and cancelled the research everyone felt would herald a new era of successful innovation - then you are perhaps not going to be the most popular person in the company.

Now there is considerable danger in making decisions in order to be popular, and I am not suggesting either that hard decisions should not be faced or should be fudged; equally there are professional troubleshooters who do nothing but this sort of thing and manage to retain a positive profile in the organisation for which they work. But one still might conclude that there are certain activities and tasks that are better avoided if your subsequent profile and career are not to be blighted. Even if the blight is small you may be better without it. It would be invidious to offer more specific advice but the point is worth keeping in mind, and should you feel exposed in this kind of way at least you can take action to rebalance the effect.

CHAPTER 9
MOVING ON

BEYOND YOUR CURRENT ROLE

Few people spend their entire career with one employer, and some of those few who do are in large multinational entities where effectively they are a conglomeration of different companies. So you may well come to the point where changing jobs is the only way you see the possibility of continuing to develop your career. This book, as you know, is not presenting a blueprint for obtaining jobs, but there are some issues here that fit our brief and are things about moving jobs you should have in mind well in advance before taking steps to do so.

CHOOSE THE RIGHT MOMENT TO GO

Get the timing wrong and the funniest story will fall flat. Get it wrong in a career and the same can happen. You need to consider this from two angles. First, when you should initiate action to seek another appointment, and secondly when it is right to take advantage of an opportunity that presents itself.

In both cases, the thinking starts with a review of the prospects within your existing situation. If you have a plan (and if you did not before then by this stage of reading through this book you should have) that is the place to start. It is likely that a new position would better enable you to reach your objectives than continued progress where you are now? You have to balance the "devil you know" against something inherently less known, but, quite possibly, no more difficult to predict. For many people the temptation to stay put and not, as they see it, take a risk is very great. On the other hand, if the offer comes to you, that always feels flattering and maybe difficult to resist as you compare a current employer where your progress is slower than you would wish, with someone who is offering an immediate change and jump in salary.

Several issues may form a part of the decision:

- *Predictability:* In some organisations formal career planning is well-spelt out. You know with reasonable certainty the kind of progress that you will likely make and you may have to balance this against something more unknown. Of course, the reverse may be the case – you have no idea what even the next year with your current employer will bring and have to put that alongside firm offers and changes from elsewhere.
- *Speed of progression:* This needs assessing separately from predictability. For example, my own move out of the publishing industry was based mostly on this factor. However well I might have done I was going to spend too long at the lower levels, not least of earnings, to suit my plan; offered something else attractive which jumped me forward, I took it. The downside of this could be that what you select produces immediate progress but then a halt; though I have no regrets.
- *Future opportunity:* One option may hold out better long term prospects than another and such decisions should always look well ahead, so far as you are able to do so.
- *Current prospect:* These need objective consideration. It is easy to underrate the situation with a current employer when faced with a new opportunity.

And of course, there is the job itself – the current one or another – and all that they entail or might entail; back to your objectives. Objectives are dynamic. You do not have to step out of education, form some plans and then never change them. Not least in a successful career where you may decide to become more and more ambitious. For example, being on the Board may not be among your aspirations early on. Then you do sufficiently well to see it as actually a real option and a move to achieve that may be exactly what you should then be planning.

It is valid too to see a move as temporary. One of the commonest examples of this is those people who work for a while overseas, or with an international company, or both, to give themselves this particular kind of experience. Also valid is to consider possible regrets if a possible course of action is not followed. Again in my own case, when I was setting up my own firm it was for all sorts of reasons, what I wanted to do.

At the same time there were also other options. Amongst everything else, the feeling that if I did not try it I would regret it forevermore ran high, made stronger by the fact that it would probably have been more difficult to do later than it was at the time (this option is rarely easy, but, in my case, so far so good!). It is no good having a reasonable job but spending your life looking back and saying to yourself, "If only I had..." You cannot wind the clock back.

Finally, another measure may be useful. It is said that if you are not going forward it is time for a change. Everyone wants a job in which they continue to learn and develop. If a job has ceased to provide this and is merely repetitive then it may be time to move on. If you have other offers consider them carefully and always remember in that case there are three options: staying, and progressing where you are, taking an offer that has arisen to go elsewhere or going out to find someone who will make you an offer. The latter could be harder work than taking something offered and there on a plate, but it could be the best bet in the long run.

If you stay too long with one organisation, you may be regarded as having limited experience (though what recruiters regard as "too long" varies a good deal). Conversely, if you have a C.V. that shows a career record of ceaseless change you may come to be regarded as a "job-hopper" and less attractive because of that. Certainly, it is quite possible that whichever your circumstance the time you spend with one employer lets your job hunting skills atrophy. Career development of the sort discussed here includes positive action to prevent this happening. Several things can be done, amongst them:

Keep your C.V. up-to-date: Most job hunting necessitates having an up-to-date statement of your background, qualifications and experience, even someone approaching you may want this, so will recruitment agencies and consultants. These quickly get out of date. It is not sufficient for them to say who you worked with and your job title, certainly for more recent jobs they should spend some of their limited space describing achievements and what you can do for someone else and how. So make notes, review the document regularly and update as necessary (computers make this much easier than in the past).

Finally, I want to make an obvious statement: you need a well-constructed and well-written C.V. – it is a selling document and there can be no half measures. It is either good enough to play its part in getting you a new job or it is useless, just so much waste paper.

Incidentally the covering letter that goes with a C.V. is also vital. In both cases, despite all the detailed published advice about them, the prevailing standards are not so high that you cannot score points and differentiate yourself by producing a really good one. Remember too that, while you may keep a standard document on file, you may need to tailor it to a particular job application.

Keep your interview skills up-to-date: This may be more difficult than editing your C.V. but anything you do infrequently tends to be more difficult than something you are able to practice. As a result, some would say it is worthwhile to apply for a job now and then not because you intend to take it (or a least not on the evidence to hand) but just to give yourself interview practice.

I am conscious of the horror this will engender in any recruiter reading this; it is difficult enough to undertake a selection campaign without the picture being clouded by a host of people practising interview techniques, so I will add that this is very much not something to be overdone; but it is a thought.

Review the press and keep in touch with agencies (on and off line): You need to know what is the state of the market, who is hiring, what rates are being paid, and this too needs an active approach.

TAKE ACTION TO MOVE THOROUGHLY AND WELL

Competition for jobs in most economies is often considerable. The points above about keeping up-to-date are part of the answer, but once you are into the process everything must be done well. This includes:

- Reading job advertisements or other job descriptions carefully
- Writing individually composed covering letters to suit the job (and sometimes tailoring the C.V. also)
- Filling in *all* of an application form and doing so clearly and thoroughly (I know much of the information is on the C.V., but recruiters find it easier to compare options presented in similar form, and so would you). Also do so honestly, the incidence of lies on such forms is high, yet who would hire someone if one such is discovered?

- Preparing for interviews
- Being punctual
- Taking the proceedings seriously
- Handling any follow-up efficiently (they may want additional information).

All this is common sense. Try to put yourself in the position of the person attempting to fill a job. It can be a thankless and difficult task, yet there is much hanging on it, the costs of getting it wrong are certainly high. They expect you to be well turned out, they recognise that few recruitment's result in the appointment of anyone who turns out to be better than was thought, though quite a few transpire the other way round. Make it easy for them to see that they are dealing with a professional, someone who will go to some pains to help them make the right decision and your success rate is likely to be higher. This is very obviously a key area, one of many details, and one where further reading is likely to be worthwhile.

ALWAYS LEAVE ON GOOD TERMS

Perhaps a seemingly small and simple point, this can prove invaluable later on; sometimes much later. No one's time in any organisation is entirely positive. You are unlikely to see eye to eye with the boss or others over everything. There will be those who always got right up your nose and others where minor niggles characterised your dealings with them. Then you leave and move on. This is not the time to indulge yourself with righteous indignation, still less revenge – even a barbed remark in a resignation letter, final report or memo may be remembered and quoted later out of context. Leave with good grace. Say something about the good things, of which there were presumably some if you have opted to stay there a while, and do not make anything even remotely like an enemy as you take your leave.

If you ask why, and the temptation for at least some throw away jibe may be great, the reason is that you never know where your ex-colleagues (and ex-boss, for that matter) will end up. They may move on too. You may need a reference, or advice or information. This is a two-way street, and it may be worth indicating to people you may find useful in future that you hope to keep in touch, and that should they think you can help them in future they should not hesitate to say so. There may be contacts that need active maintenance, people with whom you begin to network, and these need adding to any reminder system you use.

Of course, none of these should be taken as inferring that there are bound to be difficulties; there may be few or no problems as you move on. Nor that there will not be people with whom you will not easily and naturally keep up contact with on either a social or business basis, or both. That is as it should be, but during the run up to a change, and certainly during the time the change is actually taking place, it is worth a little thought to smooth the path. Do not be like an old friend of mine who landed an excellent new job and moved on. I asked him later if he had left on good terms. "Certainly," he said, "it was all fine right up to the drinks in the office on the day I left. I drank a little too much and poured a beer over the M.D's head!" You never know who will be useful in future, so never jeopardise a good relationship inadvertently or for no good reasons. Good contacts, and friendships, are too valuable to waste.

DO NOT UNDERESTIMATE THE DIFFICULTY

Countries, economies and times vary but if you have to get another job – because your contract has expired, you have been made redundant or, worse case, you have been fired – do not ever underestimate the time and effort that may be involved in obtaining a new job; certainly the right new job. If the economy is strong, employment high and skilled and experienced people are in high demand, then there may well be little problem. If not, if luck is against you, then you need to take the appropriate action and do so wisely and fast. A prolonged period of unemployment does not look good on your record and after a while, rightly or wrongly, it gets more difficult for you to interest new employers. They may, understandably, view the gap as suspicious and view other candidates more favourably.

So, what does not underestimating what needs to be done mean? An earlier section made the point about all action taken needing to be done thoroughly and well. Here the point concerns quantity. It is wisely said that searching for a job can be a full time job in itself. There is a difference between being employed and beginning to look for something new with there being no pressure to move on quickly and having to get another job before the lack of salary begins to seriously affect your life style. Make a real routine of it, set specific time aside each day (even 9 to 5) and work through all the things to be done. These will include:

- Checking all the media that carry job advertisements (websites, newspapers, management journals, trade, professional and sectional magazines)
- Contacting any appropriate recruitment agencies or consultants
- Research (some ads may look attractive, but you may not even be clear what business the organisation is in; this and other details may be worth checking)
- Writing and tailoring applications; and no doubt completing application forms
- Preparing for interviews you may obtain
- Writing on spec to specific organisations even if they are not currently advertising
- Maintaining contact systematically with your network of people who might be able to help or might know someone else who might help

- Expanding your network of contacts – now is the time to attend all those association meetings and committees that were previously difficult to fit into your diary
- Keeping up-to-date in any way necessary with the technicalities of your area of work
- Doing any simple development you can fit in (even reading a business book may be useful).

You cannot really have too many applications out there prospecting for you, and it may be worth setting yourself some targets to make sure you do put enough bread on the waters. Certainly you should never stop or slow other activities because you have your sights optimistically on one particular job, even if you are sure things are going well. Organisations can take time – weeks, sometimes months – to make a decision. If you do wait and slow down other activities, and then the answer is negative, the result is simply that you have lost time.

A systematic search will stand the best chance of getting you back into employment promptly and, after all, there is no harm in receiving more than one offer; you can always choose the best.

EXPECT THE UNEXPECTED

What we have been reviewing here is a process that can be applied over many years; so the things that will happen, the twists and turns of fate that will occur during your career will be many and varied. You can never anticipate them all. But you may well be able to take advantage of them, provided you have your wits about you.

Many things will occur. I can think of career changes in my own life influenced by factors as varied as the death of a colleague, a chance conversation, a company hitting economic difficulty, the discovery of abilities or possibilities not just which I did not know, but which I had discounted, and unexpected overseas travel. Whatever stage you are at in your career you will no doubt be able to look back on some things which have similarly already had an influence; and there will in all probability be many more to come. Be ready for them. Not specifically, you cannot know what is round the corner, but if you develop the habit of looking for opportunity in everything then some of these random factors can be made to work for you. This together with a real career plan can take you forward and, however it may all go in future, can avoid you ever having to look back and say: "If only I had done..."

AFTERWORD

"Work is much more fun than fun."
Noel Coward

However you decide to rank the most important factors in your life – home, family, partner, health – your job will rank high in the list. It takes up a very significant part of your life. If it interests you this is important, if you enjoy it and find it fun so much the better. If you can achieve all these and find something that meets whatever other list of priorities you put on it, factors as diverse as, for example, location and security, and at which you can achieve a satisfactory reward and recognition, you may be well pleased.

But, and this was said early on, *it will not just happen*. What is more, the statistics are not in your favour. Pyramid-shaped organisations, by their very nature, have more people in them at lower levels than higher ones. So career development needs working at. So too, of course, does finding a job. But it has not been the intention here to review that complete process but rather to review how exactly you can work at career development in a way that increases the chances of getting where you want more rapidly and more certainly than would otherwise be the case. I have not, in writing this book, had any preconceived idea of success in mind, certainly not seeing being Chief Executive as the only or most desirable goal. The point is to set your own objectives and then take conscious action that will get you as close as possible to those goals whatever they may be, though there are almost certainly greater dangers in aiming too low than in aiming high. Vision and ambition together are a powerful combination. Compare the personal situation with that of a company. It is said that many companies could make a success of being in the taxi business, but that only the one who defines their business more broadly as "transportation" will ever go to the moon! Sights should therefore be set reasonably high.

To achieve all these and make career development work for you there is regrettably no guaranteed magic formula. Of course, luck can and does play a part – so too can the old premise of making your own luck – but luck is not to be relied on, and just waiting for it to happen is simply not one of the options. You need to take positive action. More than that, you need to take regular, on-going action. Career development can perhaps be well described as a campaign, one that continues as long as you work, for you can never rest on your laurels. Competition is ever present and opportunities will often not wait. If you take your eye off the ball as it were, even briefly, your career prospects can change in a moment. This can result in a step back or a step forward. So what does work? Which are the things that make the difference? Many work at it a little – and hope, but others seem to get it right, in some cases consistently right and succeed sometimes beyond even their wildest dreams.

What is necessary is an all-embracing attitude to the task. You need to see all the activities in which you are involved – and a selection of them have been reviewed here, selected both to give attention to the priorities and to illustrate the range of different types of influence – in two parallel ways: in terms of how they work for you in the job you have and the tasks which that currently involves and in terms also of what effect they may have on your career. The effect you then achieve is cumulative, you build up a situation which progressively makes your career more likely to progress successfully.

Some of the inputs are small, others may be more individually significant. Together they are capable of adding up to something that can give you an edge that will get you where you want to be. And if everything you do works well, the overall effect can be very powerful. Consider one last idea:

NEVER CUT OFF YOUR OPTIONS

I think this is the most sensible and useful piece of advice I have ever been given in this area. Realistically the options you have, indeed the options you build into your career plan are more like a river constantly branching into tributaries than one straight road. There is rarely advantage in rejecting privately or taking action that rules out any particular path. Unless you are genuinely clairvoyant (in which case what are you doing reading this? You *know* what level of success you will achieve!), you never know in advance which will be the best route. Circumstances change. What seemed like a long shot suddenly becomes a real possibility, or what seems secondary becomes your best option; *provided you have not ruled it out*. So keep all your options open and only do away with any for good reason (it is possible sacrificing one will open up another, and perhaps a better one, but this should be a conscious decision). Career planning has a good deal in common with strategy. You need to take a strategic view and the rule just discussed is in fact just one aspect of this process.

FINALLY...

However it works out, whatever position you end up in, perhaps two points are more important than any others. First, that at the end of the day you feel that any success you enjoy was something you made happen, and that you have not missed taking all reasonable steps (you do not want to spend your life looking back and saying "If only...", hence the conscious and systematic approach I have advocated).

Secondly, that wherever it takes you, you enjoy the journey as much as possible. To sum up I would like to quote the journalist and columnist Katherine Whitehorn who said: "The best careers advice to give the young is: find out what you like doing and get someone to pay you for doing it." That sounds good at any age.

Finally, I will not wish you luck, after what was said earlier, but I certainly wish you well with your career, whatever it may be.

ABOUT THE AUTHOR

Anthony Jacks worked in sales, sales management and marketing before joining a management institute and then moving into consultancy and training. He was a Director of a medium-sized consultancy before setting up his own operation. He now has more than twenty-five years experience as a successful trainer, working in a wide variety of industries and in overseas markets as well as the United Kingdom. He specialises in developing communications skills such as selling, negotiation, business writing and making presentations. He has also written on a variety of business matters and is the author of *How to be Better at Marketing* (Kogan Page).

OTHER BOOKS IN THE SMART SKILL SERIES

THE SMARTER WAY TO LEARN

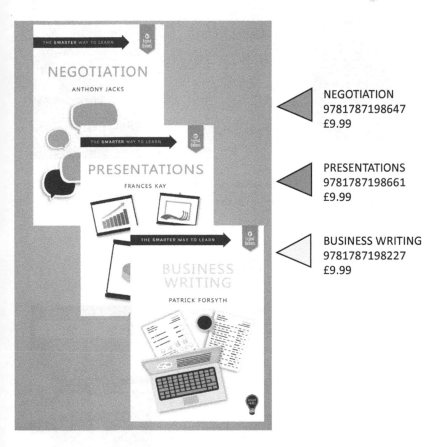

NEGOTIATION
9781787198647
£9.99

PRESENTATIONS
9781787198661
£9.99

BUSINESS WRITING
9781787198227
£9.99

The Smart Skills series, providing accessible, up-to-date and dynamic advice for all aspects of working in business, whether as an owner or executive or starting out in a first job.

Legend  Business

READ MORE

**BUSINESS GUIDE TO THE
UNITED KINGDOM 2017: BEXIT,
INVESTMENT AND TRADE**
9781785079139 • RRP £44.99

**BUSINESS PLANS THAT
GET INVESTMENT:
A REAL WORLD GUIDE**
9781785079320 • RRP £14.99

**GROWING BUSINESS
INNOVATION**
9781787198937 • RRP £39.99

**SMART SKILLS SERIES:
BUSINESS WRITING**
9781787198227 • RRP £9.99

**SMART SKILLS SERIES:
NEGOIATION**
9781787198647 • RRP £9.99

**SMART SKILLS SERIES:
PRESENTATION**
9781787198661 • RRP £9.99

**MANAGING CYBERSECURITY
RISK BOOK 1**
9781785079153 • RRP £39.99

**MANAGING CYBERSECURITY
RISK BOOK 2**
9781785079153 • RRP £39.99

OTHER BOOKS IN THE SMART SKILL SERIES

THE SMARTER WAY TO LEARN

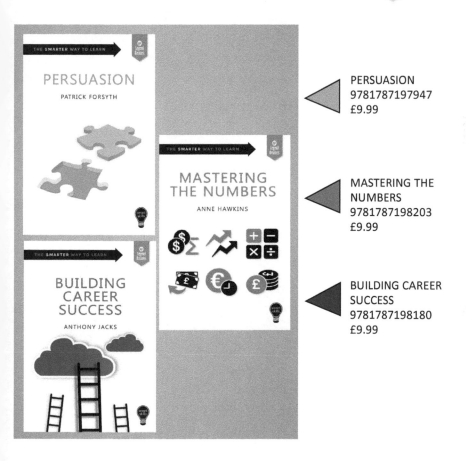

PERSUASION
9781787197947
£9.99

MASTERING THE
NUMBERS
9781787198203
£9.99

BUILDING CAREER
SUCCESS
9781787198180
£9.99

The Smart Skills series, providing accessible, up-to-date and dynamic advice for all aspects of working in business, whether as an owner or executive or starting out in a first job.